JEREMY BENTHAM; HIS LIFE AND WORK • CH ATKINSON

Publisher's Note

The book descriptions we ask booksellers to display prominently warn that this is an historic book with numerous typos, missing text or index and is not illustrated.

We scanned this book using character recognition software that includes an automated spell check. Our software is 99 percent accurate if the book is in good condition. However, we do understand that even less than one percent can be a very annoying number of typos! And sometimes all or part of a page is missing from our copy of a book. Or the paper may be so discolored from age that you can no longer read the type. Please accept our sincere apologies.

After we re-typeset and design a book, the page numbers change so the old index and table of contents no longer work. Therefore, we usually remove them.

Our books sell so few copies that you would have to pay hundreds of dollars to cover the cost of proof reading and fixing the typos, missing text and index. Therefore, whenever possible, we let our customers download a free copy of the original typo-free scanned book. Simply enter the barcode number from the back cover of the paperback in the Free Book form at www.general-books.net. You may also qualify for a free trial membership in our book club to download up to four books for free. Simply enter the barcode number from the back cover onto the membership form on the same page. The book club entitles you to select from more than a million books at no additional charge. Simply enter the title or subject onto the search form to find the books.

If you have any questions, could you please be so kind as to consult our Frequently Asked Questions page at www.general-books.net/faqs.cfm? You are also welcome to contact us there.

General Books LLC™, Memphis, USA, 2012. ISBN: 9781151246172.

JEREMY BENTHAM CHAPTER I

BOYHOOD AND EARLY YEARS

BENTHAM'S ancestors had been, for three generations at any rate, substantial London citizens of credit and renown. The great-grandfather was a prosperous pawnbroker of the time of Charles II. ; the grandfather, a flourishing attorney in the early years of the eighteenth century—" neither better nor worse," as his grandson said, "than the average rate of attorneys," who in those days were but "little thought of." Jeremiah Bentham, the father, clerk to the Worshipful Company of Scriveners, and himself a scrivener, had, by the acquisition of freehold land and leases, added largely to an already considerable patrimony. Bentham, in after years, was fond of narrating how his father used to take him, when a boy at Westminster School, to the Rainbow coffee-house, where "the *quality* of the Scriveners' Company mustered." More than once the child was allowed to be present on the occasion of the great annual festival, which was, it seems, usually preceded by a small but choice banquet for the entertainment of a select coterie: "Under the plea of catering for the many at the great dinner, the privileged few, among whom my father was, always managed to get for themselves an initiatory—a little dinner; and the Scriveners' Company paid for both. I remember when they got to turtle dinners; and the next step was to send home turtle to their wives."

Bentham's grandparents had resolved that their son should marry a young lady of their acquaintance with the comfortable jointure of some £10,000; but, much to their chagrin, the young man, at the age of thirty, fell deeply in love with one Alicia Grove, whom he had met accidentally at Buckholt Acres, a place of entertainment in or near Epping Forest. Miss Grove's father was a prosperous tradesman of Andover, and appears to have been a man of gentle birth. On his death, his widow sold the business and withdrew, with the rest of the family, to a pleasant country residence near Reading, known as Browning Hill. The Benthams, however, persisted in regarding the connection as a *m/salliance,* and Jeremy's paternal grandmother always spoke to him of his parents' marriage as a sad mistake.

The marriage took place in the autumn of 1744, and, on the 15th of February, 1748 (new style), a son was born in Red Lion Street, Houndsditch, a quarter of the town at that time still frequented by the professional classes. The boy was called Jeremy after the name of his father, though in a slightly curtailed form, on the double ground that it was shorter and, moreover, manifested a preference for the nomenclature of the New Testament over that of the Old. A second son, Samuel, who afterwards became a prominent official in the Russian service, was born some nine years later. Recognised as an able and ingenious man, Samuel acquired considerable distinction in this country as a naval architect and inventor of mechanical contrivances. He was knighted and died in 1831, the year before the death of his elder brother.

The father of these boys was an active, kindly man, capable in the conduct of affairs, and in many respects a thoughtful and affectionate parent. But, being vain and inordinately ambitious, Jeremiah Bentham utterly failed to comprehend the sensitive, retiring character of his son Jeremy, who valued intellectual treasures only. "Never," says Dr., afterwards Sir John, Bowring, "were two natures more unlike. The consequence was that Bentham never opened his heart to his father. He could not even communicate to him his sorrows." In old age the son, naturally of a happy, gay, and even jovial disposition, was wont to declare that this want of sympathy had resulted in the memories of his boyhood being overshadowed by many a gloomy thought and painful association.

Intensely proud of the child's mental powers, which were conspicuous from earliest infancy, the elder Bentham was for ever urging Jeremy to press towards the goal of worldly fame. He entirely failed to perceive that his son was born to be something better and nobler than a successful schemer for preferment in Church or State.

"While my father lived, from my birth to his death, Sir Samuel's son, George Bentham (1800-1884), was a botanist of repute; he published at Paris, in 1823, French translations of some of his uncle's works, and, also, wrote a notable book on Logic.
Bentham's biographer (1792-1872); knighted 1854.
I never gave him any ground to complain of me. Often and often have I heard from him spontaneous and heartfelt assurances of the contrary. My conduct may, indeed, have sometimes been a cause of regret and dissatisfaction to him; but on what ground? My 'weakness and imprudence' in keeping wrapt up in a napkin the talents which it had pleased God to confer on me—in rendering useless, as he averred, my powers of raising myself to the pinnacle of prosperity. The seals were mine, would I but muster up confidence and resolution enough to seize them. He was continually telling me that everything was to be done by' pushing'; but all his arguments failed to prevail on me to assume the requisite energy. 'Pushing,' would he repeat— 'pushing' was the one thing needful; but 'pushing' was not congenial to my character."

Another counsellor (whose name is not recorded) urged him to the like effect, though, happily, with no greater success: "If you mean to rise, catch hold of the skirts of those who are above you, and care nothing for those who are beneath you." Bentham at all times turned a deaf ear to the plausible doctrine of "push," and would have none of this advice; but the friend who gave it, says Dr. Bowring, caught hold of the skirts of an archbishop and became a judge. "O God, my God!" cried St. Augustine, "what misery did I then endure, what deception! For it was held up to me, as the whole duty of a boy, to obey those who exhorted me to get on in the world, and make a name in wordy arts, which minister to the glory of man and deceitful riches." i *Confessions,* Dr. Bigg's edition, at p. 45.

It was a saying of Bentham's that his family had been distinguished by virtues on the female side; and certainly all that we know of Alicia Grove—the cause of Jeremiah Bentham's matrimonial "mistake "—reveals her as a most loving, gentle creature, and devoted mother. Her husband, in his own phrase, lived with her "in a constant and uninterrupted state of nuptial happiness," while her sons entertained for her an abounding affection. Let her speak for herself. In August, 1749, when "Jerry" was eighteen months old, she writes home from Andover, whither she had gone on a visit:—

"I try to divest myself of all uneasy cares, and think of nothing at home but the joys I left behind—my sweet little boy and his still dearer papa; though there are little anxious fears about death and fever, and too great a hurry and perhaps vexations in business, which may overpower the spirits, and I not present to bear my part, and soothe those cares; which I flatter myself would be in my power, were it only from my desire of doing it. Shall you see the dear little creature again? I dreamed he had been like to have been choked with a plumstone. Surely nurse will not trust him with damsons. God preserve him from all evil accidents!"

To the tender care of this good woman who, unhappily, died just before he reached the age of eleven years, Bentham owed much, and he was ever ready to make grateful acknowledgment of the debt. Sorely did the child stand in need of a mother's fostering care. Slight and delicate of frame, he was, in stature, almost a dwarf, and so remained until, at sixteen years of age, he grew ahead. He afterwards described himself as having been "the feeblest of all feeble boys"; and used to relate how, when, as a tiny creature of seven, an attempt was made to teach him to dance, he proved to be so weak that he could not support himself upon tiptoes. "One Mr. Harris, a Quaker, offended me not a little by asking me whither my calves were gone a-grazing."

At the age of seventy-eight he pronounced himself to be stronger than he had ever been at any previous period of his life. Even in his Oxford days, a certain Goodyear St. John, "a drunken fellow who became a parson," by way of providing diversion for the company, would hold him up by the heels. "He used to take me by the heels and hold me, my head downwards; and I remember," the narrator characteristically added, " losing half a guinea in consequence, which fell out of my pocket."

The child did not suffer merely from physical weakness: he was nervous and sensitive to a painful degree. As an evidence of the acuteness of his sensibilities, he would often, when an old man, recall the fact that his earliest recollection was the pain of sympathy. It was on the occasion of some unusual feasting in the family house at Barking; he was still a mere baby unable to walk alone, and had been supplied by his nurse to satiety. Afterwards his grandfather came in and offered something more, of which the child partook: "thereupon came my mother smiling; she came with her natural claims upon my affections—but it was out of my power to accept her intended kindness; and I burst into tears, seeing the chagrin and disappointment which it cost her!"

The subject of ghosts, he declared, had always been among the torments of his life. In his boyhood it was a permanent source of amusement for the servants to ply him with horrible phantasms: every spot that could be made to answer the purpose was the abode of some spectre or another; and, seventy years afterwards, he still retained impressions created by the tricks then played upon a nervous susceptibility. "Though my judgment is wholly free," the old man would say of his ghostly fears, "my imagination is not wholly so.

"

Nothing gave the boy so much pleasure as the country delights of Browning Hill and Barking, where he spent a great deal of time with his two grandmothers. "At Browning Hill everybody and everything had a charm.... We had a garden and an orchard, bountifully productive; a large extent of stabling and out-houses; venerable elms scattered here and there offered ornament and shade; the access to the estate was over a pleasant green studded with cottages."

Hazlitt asserted that Bentham had "a great contempt for out-of-door prospects, for green fields and trees"—a curiously inaccurate statement. M. Halevy suggests that Hazlitt, in this respect, confused Bentham with James Mill; and, indeed, Bentham's sense of enjoyment of country scenes was always most acute. To use his own phrase, he was ever " passionately fond " of flowers. "So long as I retained my sense of smell," he exclaimed shortly before his death, "a wallflower was a memento of Barking, and brought youth to my mind."

For boyish amusements of the ordinary type he was entirely unfitted, alike by physical infirmity and natural disinclination; companions of his own age he had none. Referring to a later period, presumably his life at Oxford, he said, "I was a member of a cricket club, of which Historian Mitford was the hero. I was a dwarf, and too weak to enjoy it." Fishing he declared to be an abominable sport, waste of time associated with cruelty: "yet I fished; I wanted new ideas and new excitements." He had, however, neither the skill nor the strength to practise fly-fishing; and, as for shooting, although he went out once or twice with the ostensible object of destroying partridges, he disliked the pursuit, complained that the flash of the gunpowder hurt his eyes, and, thereafter, excused himself from joining in the sport, which probably had, on other grounds, become distasteful to him, for he ever shrank from the sight of animal suffering. "To my apprehension," wrote he, "every act by which, without prospect of preponderant good, pain is knowingly and willingly produced *in any being whatsoever,* is an act of cruelty; and like other bad habits, the more the correspondent habit is indulged in, the stronger it grows, and the more frequently productive of bad fruits."

The rapid and remarkable growth of the boy's mental powers afforded a striking contrast to his tardy physical development. His father was for ever "bragging" of Bentham's accomplishments: "He was always talking to me and to others of my powers." His father's friends used to call the child "Philosopher" when he William Mitford (1744-1827), brother of the first Baron Redesdale, and a contemporary of Bentham at Queen's College, Oxford. His *History of Greece* began to appear in 1784.

Letter to *Morning Chronicle,* 4th March, 1825; Bowring, x. p. 550. was only five years of age; and no biographical notice of Jeremy omits the story of his escaping one day from the company of his elders to scamper home and call for a huge folio of Rapin's *History of England.* "This," he said, "occurred before I was breeched, and I was breeched at three years and a quarter old.... The tale was often told in my presence of the boy in petticoats, who had come in and rung the bell, and given orders to the footman to mount the desk upon the table, place the folio upon the desk, and provide candles without delay." Bowring does not identify the passages selected for perusal by the student, but we have Bentham's own avowal that, whatever benefits he may have derived from the history in other respects, it was certainly of little advantage to him from a moral point of view. Rapin, he tells us, was a soldier by trade, and his history a history of throat-cutting on the largest scale for the sake of plunder; this throat-cutting and plundering being placed by him at the summit of virtue.

Such written evidence as is accessible undoubtedly supports the oral tradition as to Bentham's precocity. We may refer, for example, to certain confirmatory entries in his father's account books. Thus, in 1751, when the boy was in his fourth year, we find, " *Ward's Grammar, is. 6d.; Fani Colloquendi Formula, 6d.;* and *Nomenclator Classicus Trilinguis, 8d.:* being *2s. 8d.* for Jeremy, Junior"; while among other memoranda of the elder Bentham is treasured a line of Latin, neatly written in a child's hand, and labelled " Mem: The line pasted hereon was written by my son, Jeremy Bentham, the 4th of December, 1753, at the age of five years, nine months, and nineteen days.

One of his father's many embarrassing attempts to exhibit the boy's talents bore memorable fruit. Jeremy was dining with his father at the house of Dr. Markham, at that time headmaster of Westminster School, and afterwards Archbishop of York; a discussion took place as to what was meant by "genius," and the child, then six years of age, was required to give *his* ideas as to the meaning of the term. Bentham assured Dr. Bowring that, though he looked foolish and humbled, making no answer, the question haunted him for many a long day. Thirteen or fourteen years later, it occurred to him that *genius* was derived from *gigno,* and meant invention or production. "Have I a *genius* for anything?" he asked himself. And then, "What of all earthly pursuits is the most important?" "Legislation," was the answer given by Helv&ius, whose *De Esprit* he had just been reading. "And have I a genius for legislation?" he inquired again and again. At last the answer came, fearfully and tremblingly, " Yes."

Latin grammar and the Greek alphabet Bentham learned on his father's knee. One Thomas Mendham, a clerk, was brought in from the scrivener's office to instruct him in the rudiments of writing, and in music, an art associated with his earliest pleasures, and one which furnished him with the keenest enjoyment to the end of his days. Very soon he found himself "in possession of a fiddle in miniature, and able to scrape Foote's minuet"; whereupon, to improve his practice, a regular music master was introduced, to whom a guinea was paid for eight lessons—a course of instruction pursued until the boy was sent to school. "Mr. Bentham," wrote

Hazlitt in the *Spirit of the Age,*"relieves his mind sometimes after the fatigue of study by playing a fine old organ, and has a relish for Hogarth's prints."

At the age of seven, or thereabouts, Bentham was provided by his father with a French tutor named La Combe, who, for the sake of distinction, dubbed himself La Combe d'Avignon. *"Le pire de JMtnie Bentham"* says M. Halevy, " *n'est qu'un riche bourgeois, mais il sait et aime le francais, et r/dige son journal quotidien dans une sorte de franqais bizarre, mild de mots anglais et d'anglicismes."* From La Combe's residence in the household the boy derived much profit and no small degree of pleasure. He soon acquired a considerable familiarity with the French language, and accustomed himself to write in that tongue; indeed, he was wont to declare in later years that, as a youth, he wrote with greater facility in French than in English, for, with a limited choice of words, he scribbled boldly on, not pausing to pick or weigh the value of his phrases.

Under the strict regime of his parents, Bentham had been debarred from access to any book "by which amusement in any shape might be administered," and, though he read with avidity every work on which he could lay his hands, the restriction had been rarely relaxed until the arrival of M. La Combe, who at once introduced him to a collection of fairy tales. From these stories the child passed on to the delights of Fenelon's *Tekmachus.* "That romance may be regarded as the foundation-stone of my whole character; the starting-post from whence my career of life commenced," he said one day to Bowring: "the first dawning in my mind of the principles of utility may, I think, be traced to it." *Telemachus* was followed by Voltaire's *Life of Charles XII., General History,* and *Candide,* together with certain other examples of French literature which, it is hardly surprising to learn, somewhat startled the elder Bentham.

I 75S Jeremy was sent to board at Westminster. He was the smallest boy in the school but one, and stood in prodigious awe of Dr. Markham, who was (he says) "an object of adoration." In later years he described the doctor as a tall, portly man, but a shallow fellow withal, satisfied with Latin and Greek. "His business was rather in courting the great than in attending to the school. Any excuse served his purpose for deserting his post. He had a great deal of pomp, especially when he lifted his hand, waved it, and repeated Latin verses. If the boys performed their task well, it was well; if ill, it was not the less well. "

Westminster, according to Bentham, was at that time a wretched place for instruction. Some of the masters did little or nothing, and the boys were taught few useful and many useless things. The "horrid despotism" known as the "fagging" system was then in full force, though Bentham asserted that he himself never felt the touch of the rod at school nor knew what the pain of being punished was. Among the few agreeable "That Westminster in those days must have been a scene not merely of hardship, but of cruel suffering and degradation to the younger and weaker boys, has been proved by the researches of the Public Schools Commission."—Goldwin Smith's *Cowper* (English Men of Letters Series). memories that he retained of Westminster was his recollection of the stories told him, at night time, by his bedfellow, an amiable boy named Mitford, who in after life was able to afford him some assistance in the famous Panopticon project. In these stories, the product of Mitford's fancy, the heroes and heroines were models of kindness and beneficence, exhibiting the quality which Bentham afterwards styled "effective benevolence." "I remember," said he, "forming solemn resolutions, that, if ever I possessed the means, I would be an example of that excellence which appeared so attractive to me." Before he was eleven he was able to write letters in Greek and Latin to Dr. Bentham, the sub-Dean of Christ Church, and, on the 27th June, 1760, rather more than a year after the death of his mother, he set out with his father for Oxford, being, at the age of twelve years, entered a commoner of Queen's College in that University.

The boy returned to Westminster until the following October, and then went into residence at Oxford, where he inhabited gloomy rooms looking into the churchyard of St. Peter's-in-the-East, and covered with lugubrious hangings: "upon the two-pair-of-stairs' floor, in the further corner of the inner quadrangle, on the right hand as you enter into it from the outer door." These dismal surroundings revived Bentham's fears of ghosts, and he was made additionally miserable by the morose disposition of his tutor, one Jacob Jefferson—" a sort of Protestant monk"—whose chief care was to prevent Edward Bentham (1707-76); Canon of Christ Church, 1754; Regius Professor of Divinity, 1763. his pupil from having any enjoyment whatsoever. He prohibited even the mild amusement known as battledore and shuttlecock. The dons generally made a very unpleasant impression on the boy's mind; some were profligate, others morose, the greatest part insipid. Their mornings were spent in "useless routine," their evenings in playing cards. "We just went," he said, "to the foolish lectures of our tutors to be taught something of logical jargon." Gibbon, too, describes the fellows "or monks" of this time as supinely enjoying the gifts of the founders: "From the toil of reading, writing, or thinking, they had absolved their consciences."

The solitude and gloom of his rooms led Bentham to secure, in exchange, another set with somewhat more cheerful surroundings "on the ground floor, on the righthand side of the staircase, next on the left ? hand, as you go from the outer quadrangle to the staircase that leads to the former ones." The migration, "in consideration of the two guineas that accompanied it," was concealed from his father as though it had been a crime; he had, it seems, got two guineas "for his thirdings on account of his better furniture." Once, at least, he found himself in debt and was driven to seek the good offices of Dr. Bentham, whose intervention resulted in ten pounds being sent from home to eke out his narrow allowances.

Bentham found little delight in the society of those whom he met at Oxford. Neither at school nor at college did his father supply him with means for entertaining friends or indulging in extravagant pleasures; indeed, the son complained that he could never get money from his father but to play cards at an aristocrat's house. This was, presumably, part of the disastrously unsuccessful policy of " push." He often dined at the table of the Duke of Leeds (father of two schoolfellows) and was generally "tipped" a guinea, but it was always taken from him at home. "Only when I won money," he said to Dr. Bowring, "was I allowed to keep it; so that a passion for play was likely to be excited in me. But I was cured at Oxford, where they always forced me to pay when I lost; and, as I could never get the money when I won, I gave up the habit." As late as 31st December, 1765, there is an entry in his father's memoranda: "Lent Jerry sixpence to pay for his losses at cards."

A letter written on 30th June, 1761, throws some light on the University life of this boy of thirteen:—

"Dear Papa,—I have sent you a declamation I spoke last Saturday, with the approbation of all my acquaintances.... Even a bachelor of my acquaintance went so far as to say that he never heard but one speak a declamation better all the time he has been in college; which, indeed, is not much to say, as, perhaps, you imagine, for sure nobody can speak worse than we do here; for in short, it is like repeating so many lines out of *Propria quae maribus.* I have disputed, too, in the Hall once, and am going in again tomorrow. There also I came off with honour, having fairly beat off, not only my proper antagonist, but the moderator himself; for he was forced to supply my antagonist with arguments, the invalidity of which I clearly demonstrated.... I wish you would let me come home very soon, for my clothes are dropping off my back. Pray give my duty to grandmamma and love to dear Sammy, and represent the woful condition of one who is, nevertheless, your dutiful and affectionate son."

While at Oxford, Bentham was sent for to see the coronation of George III. , to " take a gape at the rareeshow," as he afterwards expressed it; and, in those days, "loyalty and virtue" were to him "synonymous terms." It is true that he came of a Jacobite stock; indeed, his grandfather attributed a failure to secure the clerkship of the Cordwainers' Company to his known devotion to the House of Stuart, while Jeremy himself was taught to call King Charles a martyr, and his infant affections were "'listed on the side of despotism." "But," said he, " my father subsequently, without much cost in conveyancing, transferred his adherence from the Stuarts to the Guelphs."

On the occasion of the death of George 1I., the boy had, it seems, written a copy of verses, which are still preserved. "Thirteen years had not been numbered by me when the second of the Guelphs was gathered to his fathers. Waste of time had been commenced by me at Queen's College, Oxford. Tears were demanded by the occasion and tears were actually paid accordingly." These verses were pronounced by Dr. Johnson (whose judgment may not have been unaffected by political Francis Jeffrey, who entered at Queen's thirty years later, wrote below his certificate of admission: "Hanc universitatem, taedio miserrime affectus, tandem hilaris reliqui, Ter: Kal: Jul: 1792; meque hisce obligationibus privilegiisque subduxi." (Lord Cockburn's *Life of Lord Jeffrey,* vol. i. p. 38.) bias) to be "a very pretty performance of a young man"; but Bentham himself, in later years, contemptuously described them as a mediocre performance on a trumpery subject, written by a miserable child.

In 1763 the boy undergraduate obtained his Bachelor's degree, and, in November of the same year, began to eat dinners at Lincoln's Inn, of which, after the lapse of more than fifty years, he became a bencher in 1817. In the December following his entry at Lincoln's Inn, Bentham returned to Oxford to attend the lectures of Dr. Blackstone, to whose famous commentaries on the laws of England he was afterwards to devote so much critical attention. But neither the *milieux* in which he moved nor the masters who taught him could incline him to their views. They seemed rather to arouse in him a spirit of antagonism. ' I, too, heard the lectures, age sixteen," he wrote in 1822, "and even then no small part of them with rebel ears." According to the student's own account, he immediately detected the fallacy respecting natural rights, and thought the reasoning as to the gravitating downwards of *hcereditas* illogical and futile. The lecturer he describes as formal, precise, wary, and affected; though the lectures, he admits, proved somewhat popular, attracting audiences varying from thirty to fifty.

Bentham was present at Wilkes' trial in the Court of King's Bench, where his father had secured for him one of the students' seats, of which—until the usage was These lectures were the product of the foundation of the Vinerian professorship in 1751-(Stephen's *Utilitarians,* i. p. 45.) HaWvy's *La Fermation du Radicalisme philosophique*, i. p. 25.

C abolished by Lord Kenyon—two were reserved on either side of the judge. These proceedings took place in February, 1764; and, four years later, Bentham chanced also to hear Wilkes' outlawry reversed in the same Court by Lord Mansfield, whose grace, eloquence, and fascinating tones greatly impressed him.

Shortly after the trial, his father took him to Matlock Wells (" where everything was cheap: we paid a shilling for a handsome dinner"), and thence the pair journeyed to Buxton, Bath, and other places of interest in the Midlands and in the West of England. This expedition was followed by a trip to Paris, and a long visit to a fine estate known as Yewhurst, the property of a friend of the elder Bentham named Mackreth, who was afterwards knighted and became member for Ashburton. Mackreth—an able and well-informed man, who had been, in turn, billiard-marker, waiter, and proprietor of White's club-house—had retired, while still young, with a considerable fortune and an inordinate ambition to be " considered a gentleman and admitted among the quality."

He had been fortunate in his marriage, having found favour in the sight of the daughter of the proprietor of the great neighbouring house, called Arthur's. She is described by Bentham as a woman whose face was beautiful, but her body deformed:—elegant in manners, "as if her father had been a duke."

Mackreth was mightily proud of the hospitality he William Murray (1705-1793); Lord Chief Justice, 1756.
Robert Mackreth (1726-1819); knighted 1795. Found guilty of taking advantage of a minor, 1786; of assaulting John Scott (afterwards Lord Eldon), 1792. *(Did. of Nat. Biog.,* xxxv. p. 186.) dispensed at Yewhurst, where he had a billiard-table, bowling-green, and other amusements. His guest was "kept in Elysium from day to day," greatly enjoyed the society of those who were staying with him in the house, and wandered gaily amidst all the attractions of the neighbourhood.
Bentham, however, greatly offended Mackreth by indulging in an immoderate fit of laughter at the dinnertable, immediately after his host had pronounced the name of some French dish. This breach of decorum, so Bentham declared, was not occasioned by any impropriety in his host's pronunciation, but was due entirely to his own unfortunate propensity to involuntary laughter, an infirmity which the youth had not the presence of mind to disclose—with the result that, much to his regret, he never received another invitation from Mackreth. "The fact was," said Bentham, "I had destroyed his purpose of ingratiating himself with two booby country gentlemen, who supposed I had detected him in some vulgarism."

In 1766 Bentham, now eighteen, took his Master's degree, and strutted in his new gown "like a crow in a gutter." Fine colours were, he tells us, the order of the day: "I had a pea-green coat and green silk breeches, which were first exhibited on a walk with Chamberlain Clarke, from Oxford to Faringdon. The breeches were bitterly tight." When the parliamentary election took place shortly afterwards, the fact of his being An old acquaintance of the Bentham family. He was an attorney, but ultimately became one of the new police magistrates, when Charles Abbot succeeded in passing a Bill for the creation of those functionaries.
under agp gave rise toaquestion (never definitely resolved) as to the validity of a vote which he then recorded.

It was on the occasion of his visit for the purpose of this election that he obtained, at the circulating library attached to Harper's coffee-house, near Queen's College, Priestley's *Essay on Government,* which suggested to his mind the phrase, "the greatest happiness of the greatest number." This famous formula, so he afterwards declared, discovered to him the only true standard of right or wrong, and light was thereby added to the warmth of passion already kindled in his breast for improvement in government and the melioration of the lot of mankind. At the sight of it, said he, I cried out, like Archimedes, as it were in an inward ecstasy, *JUvprjKa*! According to Bowring, Bentham stated that he had seen the phrase in one of Priestley's pamphlets so early as the year 1764, but this would seem to be *s* a mistake: the *Essay* was first published in 1768, and, in the section on Political Liberty, its author observed that "the good and happiness of the members, that is the majority of the members, of any state, is the great standard by which everything relating to that state must finally be determined." This is probably the passage to which Bentham referred.

In the following year he bade a final farewell to Oxford, and little further is known of his doings there, though he used to relate how a "talkative lady" of that city—wife of the aforesaid Dr. Bentham, "a little, in Montague's *Fragment on Government,* p. 34; *Deontology,* vol. i. p. 300: *cf.post,w.* 30, 31, 36.
Bow., x. p. 46; *Ibid.,* ii. p. 288.
significant, industrious man who had got some reputation for his spontaneous divinity lectures "—wanted him to marry her daughter; and such was her importunity that on one occasion he was obliged to escape out of the window.

Two years before his son took leave of the University the elder Bentham, much to Jeremy's vexation, had married a second time. The lady was Mrs. Abbot, widow of a Fellow of Balliol, who had, " in the spiritual routine of preferment," migrated to a college living at Colchester. Her stepson described her as a "smart and sprightly lady"; she was the mother of two boys, the younger of whom, Charles Abbot (1757-1829), became Speaker of the House of Commons and the first Lord Colchester. Hill Burton asserts that it was a "deep mortification" to "old Bentham" that his stepson, Charles—in contrast to the "dreamy" Jeremy—" bending the whole of his genius and industry to professional and political aggrandisement, rose step by step till he became Speaker of the House of Commons and was called to the House of Peers." As to this assertion, it seems sufficient to observe that Jeremiah Bentham died ten years before Abbot became Speaker, and that, when the latter was made a peer, "old Bentham " had been in his grave nearly a quarter of a century.
Benthamiana, p. xiv. CHAPTER II LIFE IN LINCOLN'S INN THE record of Bentham's life during the ten years which followed his call to the Bar, though somewhat meagre, is far from being devoid of interest. There were, he tells us, a cause or two at nurse for him, but his first thought was how to put them to death; and as his endeavours "were not altogether without success," it will readily be surmised that he made no mark in the practice of the law. His father's friend, Chamberlain Clarke, briefed him in an equity suit involving about £50. Bentham advised that the suit should " be ended and the money that would be wasted in the contest saved." "I never pleaded in public," said he; "I just opened a bill two or three times, saying a few words for form." Being set to read "old trash" of the seventeenth century, he looked up to the huge mountain of law in despair: "I can now," he declared half a century afterwards, "look *down* upon it from the heights of utility."
To a young man of vast energy and un-

usual mental activity such a condition of affairs soon became intolerable. His father, disconsolate at this want of success, had begun to regard him in the light of a lost child: "despair had succeeded to the fond hopes which something of prematurity in my progress had inspired.... I had contracted—oh! horrible!—that unnatural and, at that time, almost unexampled appetite—the *love of innovation!"*

But, eager for *reform* as he had become, Bentham never took any real interest in party politics until he was well past middle age. So far as he can be said to have professed any political faith at this period of his life, it was that of the Tories, though he declared that he did not even know what "sort of a thing" party was: he was hostile to the cause of the American colonists, owing (as he afterwards explained) to the inadequacy of its presentment by their friends in this country; the fact that Wilkes opposed the King's wishes was sufficient to render him an object of "perfect abhorrence." "I was, however (he told Bowring many years later), a great reformist; but never suspected that the people in power were against reform. I supposed they only wanted to know what was good in order to embrace it."

He was already collecting materials for a treatise designed to assail the "lawless science of the law" under the title of *Critical Elements of Jurisprudence;* he also contemplated, in the form of *A Comment on the Commentaries,* a comprehensive attack upon the recently published treatise of Mr. Justice Blackstone, whose doctrines had aroused in him such keen antagonism while yet a boy at Oxford. Blackstone, he asserted in his commonplace book, carried the disingenuousness of the hireling advocate into the chair of the Professor: "He is the dupe of every prejudice and the abettor of every abuse. No sound principles can be expected from that writer whose first object is to defend a system. "

Pending the execution of these formidable undertakings, he avowed himself powerless to pursue the practice of his profession with any hope of profit or success—" like David," said he, " I can give no melody in my heaviness." The Daemon of Chicane had, we are told, already appeared in all his hideousness, and war had been declared against him.

On the 14th of October, 1772, he writes to his father, "In the track I am in I march up with alacrity and hope; in any other, I should crawl on with despondency and reluctance." Accordingly, after much entreaty, Jeremiah Bentham gave a grudging consent; the son abandoned all pretence of active practice at the Bar and bade farewell to the brawling courts and dusty purlieus of Westminster. He continued, however, to occupy residential chambers in Lincoln's Inn, engaged for the most part with his inquiries into the principles of legislation and in chemical research.

In a fervent, flamboyant passage occurring in his commonplace book of 1774—5, Bentham proclaimed himself to be deaf to the calls of present interest and unmoved by the alluring prospects of a successful career Jeremiah Bentham has been denounced as "authoritative, restless, aspiring, and shabby." *(Edin. Review,* vol. lxxviii. p. 464.) Jeremy himself referred to his "hectoring"and "self-ostentation." *(Hal.,* i. p. 297.) But he was an affectionate and, in many respects, an excellent father. Sir Leslie Stephen asserts that "Bentham's dislike of his stepmother increased the distance between him and his father" *(Utii.,* i. p. 174),though "dislike" would seem, in the circumstances, somewhat too strong a term.
at the Bar. "Oh, Britain! Oh, my country! the object of my waking and my sleeping thoughts! whose love is my first labour and greatest joy—passing the love of woman—thou shalt bear me witness against these misruling men. I cannot buy, nor will I ever sell my countrymen. My pretensions to their favour are founded not on promises, but on past endeavours— not on having defended the popular side of a question for fat fees, but on the sacrifice of years of the prime of life—from the first dawnings of reflection to the present hour—to the neglect of the graces which adorn a private station; deaf to the calls of present interest, and to all the temptations of a lucrative profession." The first eminence at the Bar, and the opulence which attends it, were at his command (wrote Sir Samuel Romilly in 1817); and if he could have persuaded himself to accommodate his political principles to the wishes of those in power, the most splendid station and the highest honours would have been infallibly within his reach. "From those brilliant prospects he voluntarily turned away.. .. A citizen of the world in its purest sense, he has suffered no opportunity, which has presented itself, of benefiting his fellowmen in any portion of the globe, to pass away without endeavouring to improve it."
The young man's tastes were simple and his habits regular. "As soon as he had risen in the morning," wrote his friend and admirer, Brissot, "he took a long *Edin. Review,* vol. *xxix.* p. 218.
Brissot was guillotined in 1793; it was of him that Madame Roland said: "Under despotism he advocated freedom; amidst tyranny he fought for humanity. " (Bow., x. p. 191.) walk of two or three hours, when he returned to his solitary breakfast; he then applied himself to his favourite work until four in the afternoon, at which hour he always went to dine with his father." The father's income was large, but Bentham himself lived in a very economical manner; and indeed, although his passion for reading involved him in considerable expenditure on books, his means did not admit of much extravagance. On the occasion of his second marriage, Jeremiah Bentham had settled on Jeremy a small farm in Essex, producing (after payment of an excessive land tax) something under £50 a year, together with a malt-house at Barking, which, when tenanted, yielded another *£40. "*And for these allowances," he used to say, " I was to appear as a gentleman, with lace and embroidery on occasion. I had four guineas to pay my laundress, four guineas to my barber, and two to my shoeblack. " He seems, however, to have received in addition to these allowances, two or three trifling legacies, and he managed somehow, every long vacation, to de-

fray the expenses of a visit to the country in company with his friend George Wilson.

The first composition actually published by Bentham was in the form of letters addressed to the *Gazetteer* signed *Irenaeus*. They were written about 1770, to repel an attack upon Lord Mansfield, whom, at that time, he greatly admired: "I was deluded," said he to Bo wring, "by his eloquence, and fascinated by his courtesy of character." In those days composition was "inconceivably difficult" to him—he began sentences which he could not complete; he wrote on blotting-paper scattered fragments which he kept to be filled up when in happier vein; he put scraps away in drawers so that he could tumble them over and over; he was at pains to turn and polish his phrases, and in one of his earlier commonplace books is inserted the following caution:— "Having found some word, however improper, to fix the idea (upon the paper), you may then turn it about and play round it at your leisure. Like a block of wood, which, when you have fixed in a vice, you may plane and polish at your leisure; but, *if you think to keep it in your hands all the time,* it may slip through your fingers."

By hard labour, as he explained fifty years later, he subjugated the difficulties that beset him, and his example will serve to show what hard labour can accomplish; indeed, the style of his earlier writings is marked by singular care, precision and polish. "I had not then," said he, " invented any part of my new lingo. " In after life he *sacrificed everything to precision,* telling Bowring that the first duty of a writer was to leave no doubt of his meaning—he, accordingly, invented words, some of them admirable ones, whenever he found none existing in the language which exactly represented the idea he wished to convey; such as *maximise, minimise, international, forthcomingness, codification.*

Cursory readers complain that Bentham's later works, and, indeed, some of the earlier ones, abound in tedious reiterations and embarrassing intricacies; but (as his biographer, with much justice, urges on his behalf) the object of the author was to *demonstrate,* without taking "A Benthamiana might be made of passages worthy of Addison or Goldsmith." (John Mill's *Early Essays,* Gibbs' edition, p. 381.) anything for granted, so that those who would judge of the legitimacy of his conclusions must needs examine the chain of reasoning link by link, as in following the proof of some Euclidian theorem. "We can regard in no other light than that of a public misfortune," wrote Sir Samuel Romilly in the *Edinburgh Review* for November, 1817, "whatever prevents his writings from being known, and their utility and importance from being universally acknowledged. What principally obstructs their circulation is the style in which they are composed... English literature hardly affords any specimens of a more correct, concise, and perspicuous style than that of the *Fragment on Government* or the *Protest against Law Taxes*.. . Since those publications, he seems, by great effort and study, to have rendered his style intricate and his language obscure." The truth is that, while the precise meaning of a sentence is rarely involved in the slightest obscurity, its construction is often such as to demand the closest attention on the part of the reader; the whole of the qualifying remarks which he intended to make he insisted upon embedding as parentheses in the very middle of the sentence itself. Eminent critics have affIrmed that throughout Bentham's writings there are numberless passages which, in point of wit, eloquence, and expressive clearness, have rarely been excelled in the works of any writer of our Vol. xxix. p. 236: "I have spoken of Bentham," said Romilly in his Diary, "with all the respect and admiration which I entertain of him, but I have thought myself bound not to disguise his faults. I shall be extremely concerned if what I have said should give him any offence"; and *ef. Quarterly Review,* vol. xviii. p. 128.

Mill's *Early Essays,* by Gibbs, p. 381.

language: his close and ingenious reasoning provides constant and useful exercise for the mind, while his wealth of apt illustration, drawn from an infinite variety of sources, affords agreeable relaxation and enlivens the dullest topic. At the same time it is beyond dispute that men, who assuredly would not be deterred from the study of Bentham by the mere abstruseness of his subject-matter, have often been repelled by the difficulties of his later style. Francis Place, a devoted disciple, hoped to appease the severity of the master's method, and, in a letter to James Mill (October 20, 1817), observed that most men think it trouble enough to study the subject itself without being obliged at the same time to make a study of the phraseology of the author. Mill, however, betrayed great alarm on receipt of the letter, and told Place that he had not dared to read it to Bentham:—"There is no one thing (wrote Mill) upon which he plumes himself so much as his style, and he would not alter it if all the world were to preach to him till Domesday."

It must not be supposed that, at any period of his life, Bentham indulged in mere abstract theories or metaphysical reasonings. He was ever bent on some *practical* application of that principle of utility which was to him the fount of all true wisdom, a very tree of life more precious than rubies: for speculative inquiry he cared little, except, indeed, when the pursuit of such inquiry became necessary to secure the practical results at which he aimed. "He found the philosophy of law a chaos, he left it a science; he found the practice of the

Wallas' *Life of Francis Place,* p. 85.

law an Augean stable, he turned the river into it which is mining and sweeping away mound after mound of its rubbish. " In these words John Mill proclaimed the great task which his master had accomplished; how he had brushed aside the accumulated cobwebs of centuries, how he had untied knots which the efforts of the ablest thinkers, age after age, had only drawn tighter.

The science of law was founded by Bentham on this *principle of utility,* which he regarded, moreover, as the only sure foundation of the science of morals. "The right end of all human action is," said he, " the creation of the

largest possible balance of happiness "; and this tendency to produce happiness is what he meant by utility. His conception of " happiness," in the sense of a "sum of pleasures," was, writes Dr. Albee, in all respects identical with that of his Utilitarian predecessors; while his adoption of the "greatest happiness" formula was, in no sense, a departure from the traditional view of the Utilitarians, that the motive of the agent is uniformly egoistic2 In a letter to Dumont, dated 6th September, 1822, Bentham states that he took the principle of utility from Hume's *Essays:* "Hume was in all his glory, the phrase was consequently familiar to everybody. The difference between me and Hume is this: the use he made of it was to account for that which *is,* I to show what *ought to be."* Years before the date of this letter, Bentham had noted in his commonplace book that *Priestley* was the first (unless it was Beccaria) who taught his lips to pronounce the sacred *Early Essays,* by Gibbs, pp. 360, 361.
Albee's *History of English Utilitarianism* (1902), at p. 189.
MSS., Univ. Coll., No. 10; cited Hal., i. p. 282.
truth, that *the greatest happiness of the greatest number is the foundation of morals and legislation* But this apparent inconsistency seems to be explained by a remark he made one day to Bowring: "I was at fault myself when I stumbled upon *utility;* and *this was imperfect* until I found *greatest happiness* in Priestley, who did not turn it into a system and knew nothing of its value. He had not connected with happiness the ideas of pleasure and pain."
It must be allowed that Bentham was not a profound student of ethics, or economics, or of what he called psychology; but, in the opinion of John Mill, he was a great *reformer* even in philosophy, inasmuch as it was he who, beyond all others, aroused the questioning spirit, the disposition to demand the *why* of everything: "It was not his *opinions,* in short, but his *method,* that constituted the novelty and the value of what he did."

At a very early age he had dreamed of founding " a school," of controlling pupils who should be initiated in his "principles," and execute, under his eyes, various parts of his " plan." In this way he hoped to propagate his ideas and advance the publication of his writings.

George Wilson, afterwards leader of the Norfolk Circuit, was his "bosom friend" and one of his first disciples. They met at the table of Wilson's relative, Dr. Fordyce, whose lectures on chemistry were attended Bow., x. p. 142. The phrase occurs in Hutcheson's *Enquiry,* 5th ed., 1753, at p. 185; see Montague's *Fragment on Government,* p. 34 *n. Ibid.,* p. 567; *vide ante,* p. 20.
Early Essays, by Gibbs, pp. 329, 336.
MSS., Brit. Mus., 33,538, f. 222; cited Hal., i. p. 297. 1736-1802. Physician at St. Thomas's Hospital, 1770-1802. by Bentham. Wilson, we are told, was a man of clear understanding, deeply versed in the law, over six feet high, bashful and cold in manners, a most determined Whig, and "a slave to the fashion." But he soon became a great admirer of the young reformer, whom he persistently pressed to publish some of the rapidly accumulating manuscripts. The two men, indeed, lived constantly together, and once, while bathing at Leyton during a summer holiday, Wilson saved Bentham's life. On one occasion only is it recorded that there was anything approaching a quarrel between them. Wilson, it seems, told his friend that he wished to consult him on a point of law, but Bentham laughed at the suggestion. *"He* was a lawyer of eminence: / had quitted the law; he took it in dudgeon, even after I had explained it, though the explanation was simple enough." Under Wilson's cold and reserved exterior there lay the warmest attachment to his friends, and the tenderest sympathy for the misfortunes of others that I ever met with, said Sir Samuel Romilly: if judgeships were elective, and the Bar—that is, the men best able to estimate the qualifications of a candidate—were the electors, he would, by their almost unanimous suffrages, have been raised to the Bench. But, continued Romilly, judicial stations were, in those days, reserved for men who held political principles less liberal than those which Wilson entertained. After leading the circuit for some years he took silk, and retired to his native country, Scotland, where he died in 1816.
Another intimate friend of Bentham's was a certain John Lind, commoner of Balliol, who, " having received the Holy Ghost, as much of it at least, whatever it be, as the bishop could give him," became chaplain in the Embassy at Constantinople. Dismissed from the chaplaincy "for being too agreeable to his Excellency's mistress," Lind, during the year 1773, returned to England, having in his charge Prince Stanislaus Poniatowski, who had been sent upon his travels by his ill-fated uncle, Stanislaus, the last King of Poland. "The reverend divine, with the black garb and clerical wig, was now transformed into the man of fashion, with his velvet satin-lined coat, embroidered waistcoat, ruffles of rich lace, and hair dressed *d la mode'.*
' He became practically the resident of Poland at the Court, though, being a subject of the King of England, he could not be received as the representative of a foreign potentate.

As the author of a book entitled *Letters concerning the Present State of Poland,* describing the "atrocity" of the first partition, Lind acquired considerable celebrity. Aided by his commissions and address, says Bentham, the work acquired for him high and favourable notice; he was well received by the Prime Minister, Lord North; "he was well received, too, at the house of his Honourable and Right Reverend Brother, and at the card table of his not less Reverend Wife. He was rather too much at that table; sometimes I have seen him returning from it with a tolerably well-filled purse, but too often with an empty one." On more Bow., i. p. 247. Lind was born 1737 and died 1781. Brownlow North *1741-1820);* Bishop of Lichfield 1771; translated to Worcester 1774; to Winchester 1781. D than one occasion he dined at Lord Mansfield's, where, said he, the conversation was always better than the cheer.

While "in the sunshine of official favour," he produced another work, entitled *Review of the Acts of the Thirteenth Parliament, etc.* (1775). The latter book was confined in its scope to the Acts affecting the Colonies, and, indeed, to those statutes which bore directly upon the contest with America—then the question of the hour. "The plan of the argument," wrote Bentham in 1827, "he had from me. Upon his mentioning the American part of his design, his plan not being as yet formed, I told him I had written two or three pages on the subject, which, such as they were, he was welcome to do what he pleased with.... My surprise was not small at finding that this page or two of scattered thoughts had been set in front of his work, and constituted the plan on which he was operating. They form pages 15 and 16 in the printed book." This work of Lind's was written on the Government side, in support of the war, and appears to have brought Bentham to the favourable notice of Lord Mansfield, who, however, made no advance towards a personal acquaintance with the young man.

In 1774 Bentham had published a translation of Voltaire's *Le Taureau Blanc,* of which he sent a copy to his brother. Keep the sad, wicked book close, he wrote, unless you should chance to meet with one of us, and even then you must use discretion: "Remember the sage Mambres preaches up discretion—and Bow., x. p. 62.

whatever you do, let it not be known for mine." Lind addressed to the translator a letter, in the handwriting of an old man, purporting to come from Voltaire *"d son chateau de Ferney, ce 20 juillet, 1774."*

Bentham's first work of any importance appeared in 1776, and took the form of destructive, if somewhat captious, criticism applied to certain doctrines of constitutional law recently expounded by Blackstone in his *Commentaries on the Laws of England.* The book was called *A Fragment on Government:* it consisted, in fact, of a selection detached from manuscripts in course of compilation for the proposed *Comment on the Commentaries,* and was, primarily, intended to refute the doctrine of "original contract," to which Locke and his disciples adhered. While admitting the "enchanting harmony" of his author's numbers, the critic assailed the spirit of hostility shown towards "that Liberty which is Reformation's harbinger." The Tory doctrine of passive obedience forbade resistance to kingly authority, in any case, on pain of divine displeasure: the object of the Whig fiction of an "original contract," entered into between the monarch and the people, was to combat this doctrine. "The People, on their part, promised to the King a *general obedience:* the King, on his part, promised to *govern* the People in such a *particular* manner always as should be subservient to their happiness ": such was the alleged compact. "The invention was a most unhappy one," wrote MSS., Brit Mus., 33,537, ff. 288-9 and 296-7. Cited by HaleVy (i. p. 287), who adds: *"Vinfluence du style voltairien mus parafl indiscutablc dans tens Us manuscrits frattfais de Bentham."*

Bentham: "the reasonable use of occasional resistance wanted not the support of any system; and this system was not capable of supporting anything." He, accordingly, declared emphatically against the fiction, asserting that *utility* was the test and measure of all virtue; that the obligation to minister to general happiness was an obligation paramount to, and exclusive of, any other. His fundamental axiom was that the greatest possible happiness of the greatest possible number is the measure of right and wrong; deeming that to be *useful* which, taking all times and all persons into consideration, leaves a *balance of happiness*—"a principle," writes Sir Leslie Stephen, "which to some seemed a barren truism, to others a mere epigram, and to some a dangerous falsehood." As we have already seen *ante,* p. 30), Bentham informed Dumont that he "took" the principle from Hume; though we find that as early as 1769 he was reading Montesquieu and Helvtius; and, in old age, he told Dr. Bowring that Montesquieu, Barrington, Beccaria, and Helv£tius—but most of all Helvtius—"set him on" the Utility or Greatest Happiness principle.

The *Fragment* further assailed, with singular force and perspicuity, the theory of constitutional government adopted in the *Commentaries* as the philosophic basis of those ingenious and plausible reasonings whereby the English Constitution is presented to the reader as the perfection of human wisdom. In Blackstone's view, this best of all possible governments was a happy blend MSS., Univ. Coll., No. 100; cited Hal., i. p. 416.

Bow., i. pp. 17, 227. *Utilitarians,* i. p. 178. Cf. *English Local Government,* by Redlich and Hirst (1903), i. p. 70. of the monarchical, the aristocratical, and the democratical—the several branches being represented by King, Lords, and Commons. "Here, then," says he, " is lodged the sovereignty of the British Constitution; and lodged as beneficially as is possible for society." He did not even stop short at the assertion—of which Bentham readily disposed—that the three powers, charged with the legislature of the kingdom, are *"entirely independent* of each other." To this ideal scheme of Mixed Government — acclaimed by Montesquieu, adorned and extolled by Blackstone—the test of "utility" was applied: weighed in the balances, it was found to be wanting; and Bentham's exposition remains a model of forceful reasoning and critical acumen.

So early as 1775 Bentham had written the manuscripts from which Dumont, many years later, compiled the *Thforie des Peines;* and in June, 1777, we find him still very busy with the general theory of Punishments. "Wilson and I dined with Dr. Fordyce the day before yesterday; and I read him the physiological part of my Punishments, and got from him some useful corrections."

During the following spring he published a pamphlet entitled *View of the Hard Labour Bill,* exhibiting a special application of the cardinal principles of his theory of punishments to the organisation of a regular penitentiary system, and in particular to the scheme of a Bill then before Parliament, which had been introduced by William Eden, with the approval of Mr.

Letter to his brother, 4 June; MSS., Brit.

Mus., 33,538, f. 129; cited Hal., i. p. 294.

'First Lord Auckland *(1744-1814); vide post,* p. 71.

Justice Blackstone. The scheme under the Bill comprised a plan of the architecture and management of a prison for the confinement of convicts, and of this plan Bentham's tract contained a detailed and somewhat severe criticism, though he afterwards maintained that the general tone of his comments was intended to be laudatory. "My delight at seeing symptoms of ever so little a disposition to improvement, where none at all was to be expected, was," said he, " sincere and warmly expressed." Under date 5th April, 1778, the following entry occurs in Jeremiah Bentham's diary:—" *Chez fils* Jeremy, when he gave me six copies of his book to send to some of the judges by Thomas." Jeremy's comment on this entry, fifty years later, was: "In these matters I had no option. It was *pushing, pushing,pushing;* none of them took any notice of the book." Mr. Justice Blackstone, however, appears to have sent him a civil note, describing the tract as "ingenious," and adding "that some of the observations had already occurred to the patrons of the Bill, and many more were well deserving their attention." The Bill became an Act in 1779, and provided for the erection of two penitentiaries, over which John Howard (1726-90)—who, in Bentham's phrase, died "a martyr after living an apostle"—was intended to have the supervision. A site was chosen at Battersea, but the Act was never carried out, and the failure of this scheme led to the Bow., i. p. 255.

The date 1789, given Bow., xi. p. 98, is erroneous. That was the date of publication of the *Introduction,* not of the *View of the Hard Labour Bill.* The Act is 19 Geo. 3, c 74. Stephen's *Utilitarians,* i. p. 106. formation of Bentham's great "panopticon" project which, years afterwards, brought so many disasters upon its author.

He was anxious to see some general plan of punishment adopted by which solitary confinement would be combined with labour; and Howard's revelations as to the state of the prisons made his "wish still more earnest." But thirty years after Eden's projected reform—on 23rd November, 1812—Mr. Justice Chambre told Romilly that the judges frequently sentenced men to long terms of transportation—longer than they otherwise would do, or than they thought the crimes deserved—in order to secure the actual transportation of the prisoners. It was, said the learned judge, very usual, *where the prisoner was sentenced only to seven years' transportation, not to transport him at all, but to keep him for the whole term on board the hulks*—a form of punishment which, according to Mr. Justice Bailey, made the prisoners much worse than it found them!

The Soctete' Economique of Berne had, in 1777, offered a prize of fifty louis for the best plan of a Code of Criminal Law—a further sum of like amount was added by Voltaire and Thomas Hollis. Voltaire issued a commendatory pamphlet and, after some delay, Bentham resolved to compete. He set to work about September, 1778, and, in the following March, addressed to the Socidte" a letter containing the plan of his proposed Code. He appears, however, to have been too Romilly's *Memoirs,* iii. p. 71. Hal., i. pp. 140, 294.

MSS., Brit Mus., 33,538, f. 313-14 » abstracted Hal., i. p. 295. late to take part in the competition; and, though he continued to work upon the Code, his rate of progress was painfully slow. George Wilson was always ready to apply a much-needed stimulus, but, unfortunately, there was little response: "*La raison est"* explained Wilson in a letter written in French to Samuel Bentham, *"qu'il fait trop de choses à la fois, non qu'il est oisif. Il commence à /crire du Code, mais dans une heure il /crit sur vingt autres sujets, et tout cela pour ne pas perdre des id/es qui se pr/senteraient sans doute de nouveau, et qu'il a peut-être déjà dans des papiers il y a longtemps écrits et oubliés."* At last, in 1780, as a first step towards the publication of the suggested "penal Code," Bentham sent to the Press a number of manuscripts which were printed, but not then published. After an interval of nine years, with "a patch at the end and another at the beginning," they appeared as a separate work under the title of *An Introduction to the Principles of Morals and Legislation?*

On the publication, in 1776, of the *Fragment on Government,* as the work of an anonymous author, it had attracted considerable notice. The Solicitor-General, Wedderburn (1733-1805), shook his head at the mention of the principle of " utility," and declared it to be a dangerous one. The man was a shrewd man, wrote Letter 18 January, 1780; Add. MSS., Brit, Mus.; cited Hal., i. p. 296.

Bentham to Lord Wycombe, letter I March, 1789. (Bow., x. p. 197.) *Vide post,* p. 94. Why, asks M. Halévy, did Bentham leave the most fundamental portion of his work unprinted? He answers thus: *"Parce que, dans sa prioccupation de donner au droit la forme aune système intigral, aun code, il si sent isolé dans son propre pays. L'idie de codifier les lois est une idée continentale, non britannique "* (i. p. 153).

Bentham in 1822, and knew well enough what he meant, though at that time I did not. "In a Government which had for its end in view the greatest happiness of the greatest number, Alexander Wedderburn might have been Attorney-General and then Chancellor; but he would not have been Attorney-General with £15,000 a year, nor Chancellor with a peerage, with a veto on all justice, with £25,000 a year, and with sinecures at his disposal, under the name of Ecclesiastical Benefices, besides *et ccBteras"* In 1780 Wedderburn had become Chief Justice of the Common Pleas, with the title of Lord Loughborough, and in 1793 had secured the Chancellorship—an office which he held until 1801, when he retired as Earl of Rosslyn. The greatest happiness of the ruling few was the end that *he* always had in view, said Bentham; who, elsewhere, speaks of him as a cold, starched fellow—frigid and proud. Though of evil repute as a profligate politician, he was, it is said, an accomplished courtier and graceful orator. Bentham was astounded by the brilliance of the memorable onslaught on Franklin; he maintained, however, that even "after he had a silk gown on his back," Wedderburn's speech had been tongue-tied and hesitating. Churchill, too, who satirised him as—

"A pert, prim prater of the Northern race,
Guilt in his heart, and famine in his face,"

describes him as "Mute at the Bar and in the Senate loud." But Gibbon, on the other hand, praises his "skilful eloquence"; while Thurlow, who heartily despised him as a "damned Scotchman" and "no lawyer," admitted that he had "the gift of the gab." When the *Fragment* first appeared, it was by some attributed to the pen of Lord Mansfield, by others to that of Lord Camden; and it would, doubtless, have had an even greater vogue but for the premature disclosure of the authorship by Jeremiah Bentham, in a moment of paternal pride. This disclosure served to check the demand for the book—"concealment had been the plan, how advantageous, has been already visible. Promise of secrecy had accordingly been exacted; parental weakness broke it. No longer a great man, the author was now a nobody" *post,* p. 73).

In these days Bentham belonged to a dinner club, known as St. Paul's Churchyard Club, of which "the Despot" was Dr. Johnson—"pompous vamper of commonplace morality," as he was irreverently described by the younger member. Johnson "fathered" the *Fragment* on Dunning (1731—1783), the famous leader of the King's Bench Bar, who some five years after, wards became the first Lord Ashburton; a conjecture which certainly did not argue a very close acquaintance with John Dunning's mental qualities. The young author was, it is true, a profound admirer of the great advocate's forensic style, which he declared it would have given him the highest satisfaction to be able, in any way, to imitate. But beyond the possibility of some suggestion of Dunning's style, there appears to have been nothing to support Johnson's conjecture, Solicitor-General 1767-70; appointed on the resignation of Sir Ed. Willes while still wearing a stuff gown, "for no Chancellor was to be found sufficiently careless of royal resentment to allow the Counsel of Wilkes to take silk." (Lord E. Fitzmaurice's *Life of Shelbume,* ii. pp. 79-8-) which, according to Bentham, proved the collateral fact that "not only the affections, but the acquirements of the pre-eminent lawyer who was the subject of it, were altogether unknown to the miserable and misery-propagating ascetic and instrument of despotism by whom it was delivered. In the *Fragment* marks of some little general acquaintance with the field of science and general literature may be seen here and there peeping out. The office of his father—a country attorney, whose abode was in the little town from which the son, on his elevation, took the title—had been the university of John Dunning. Whatever analogy may, in respect of certain faculties, have had place between the illustrious advocate and the obscure reformist—in respect of feelings and wishes with relation to the universal interest, nothing could be much more opposite."

The disclosure of his name as that of the author of *The Fragment* brought to Bentham's garret in Lincoln's Inn a distinguished visitor in the person of Lord Shelburne. A novel, nor that altogether an uninteresting one, said Bentham many years afterwards, might be made out of a correct and unvarnished picture of the incidents to which that visit gave birth: "Fifty years hence, if I have nothing else to do, I will set about it." William Fitzmaurice (1737-1805) had succeeded to the earldom of Shelburne in 1761; educated at Christ Church, he attended with great regularity and, as he conceived, much profit to himself the Oxford lectures of the " Commentator," whom he afterwards befriended Bow., i. p. 241.

Burton attributes the visit to the publication of the *Introduction* (Benthamiana, p. 15), but that did not occur until 1789. and introduced to George III. Indeed, he made the monarch sit to be lectured by the professor: "the lecturer, as anybody may see, showed the King how Majesty is God upon earth"—wrote Bentham—"Majesty could do no less than make him a judge for it... if tailoring a man out with God's *attributes* is blasphemy, none was ever so rank as Blackstone's. " Shelburne's visit to Lincoln's Inn took place during the summer of 1781, the year after Blackstone's death—and Bentham had a notion that it had been deferred owing to the friendship between "the Lord and the Commentator. " However this may be, there had, in fact, been some slight communication between Bentham and his visitor during Blackstone's lifetime, the intermediary being Francis Maseres. Bentham, it seems, had been anxious to obtain letters of introduction for his brother, who was about to leave for Russia, and on June 16th, 1779, Maseres wrote to him: "Lord Shelburne is a goodnatured, affable man and easy of access." But there was no personal intercourse until the interview of 1781, which was soon followed by a short return visit to Shelburne House; and that, again, by an invitation to Bowood, Lord Shelburne's beautiful seat in Wiltshire— a notable event, destined to affect in a remarkable degree Bentham's after life and fortunes. Fitzmaurice's *Life of Sheliurrte,* i. p. 19. Bow., i. p. 249. *1731-1824.* One of the most honest lawyers England ever saw, said Bentham; appointed Cursitor Baron of the Exchequer 1773, he held that office for more than fifty years. "Baron Maseres who walks (or did till very lately) in the costume of the reign of George the Second": (Lamb's Essay on the *Old Benchers of the Inner Temple).* He was, moreover, Fourth Wrangler and a mathematician of considerable repute. Add. MSS., Brit. Mus. ; cited Hal., i. p. 362. CHAPTER III BENTHAM AT BOWOOD

"T MET," said Bentham, "with all sorts of rebukes A and disappointments till I was asked to Bowood." On arrival at that hospitable mansion, in August, 1781, he received a most cordial welcome from his host: "My lord came in, he ran up to me, and touched one of my cheeks with his and then the other. I was even satisfied with it, since he meant it kindly, and since such, I suppose, is the fashion; but I should have been still better satisfied if he had made either of the ladies his proxy." The ladies herein referred to were his hostess and her mother's stepdaughter, Miss Caroline Vernon. "The one," he wrote to George Wilson, " is loveliest of matrons, the other of virgins: they have both of them more than I could wish of reserve, but it is a reserve of modesty rather than of pride."

Throughout his long visit of many weeks' duration, he Lord Shelburne had from 1766 to 1768 held the seals of a Secretary of State under Chatham, acting as Colonial Minister. In 1765 he married Lady Sophia Carteret, daughter of Lord Granville; she died 1771. In 1779 he married Lady Louisa Fitzpatrick, daughter of the Earl of Upper Ossory; her sister, Lady Mary, married Stephen, second Lord Holland. (Fitzmaurice's *Shelburne,* vol. i. p. 319; ii. pp. 2, 163; iii. p. 53.) A daughter of Richard Vernon, with whom Lady Shelbume's mother had contracted a second marriage.
was, to use his own words, caressed and delighted. Lord Shelburne, he declared, raised him from the bottomless pit of humiliation; the affections he found in that heart and the company he met in that house first encouraged him to pursue and develop those vast schemes for the advancement of mankind which were already taking definite shape in his mind. "Of esteem, not to speak of affection"—said Bentham in his old age—"marks more unequivocal one man could not receive from another than in the course of about twelve years I received from Lord Shelburne." The days spent at Bowood were the happiest of his life: Lady Shelburne was "gentle as a lamb," talked French and understood Latin; while her husband, albeit of an imposing and dignified manner, was at heart generous and sympathetic, ready to catch hold of the most imperfect scrap of an idea and fill it up—" sometimes erroneously," adds Bentham, who regarded want of clearness as his host's chief mental defect. If we are to believe Dr. Bowring, Bentham, indeed, described Lord Shelburne as giving utterance to "vague generalities in a very emphatic way, as if something grand were at the bottom, when, in fact, there was nothing at all"; but Bowring (observes Sir Leslie Stephen) had a natural dulness which distorted many matters transmitted through him, and it certainly seems unlikely that one, who entertained for Lord Shelburne such affectionate regard, could have formed so unjust an estimate of his powers. Writing after Shelburne's death, Bentham portrayed him as a man "greedy of power," but endowed with such fixed *Utilitarians,* i. p. 188. intellectual principles as enabled him to make a beneficial use of it. "I wish," his lordship one day said to Mirabeau, "that convicted criminals were questioned, in order that they might be philosophically studied, after having been magisterially examined with a view to their conviction. *We govern men but we do not know them— we do not even endeavour to know them?* "There was force and character, if there was not real genius, in Shelburne's oratory," wrote Lord Holland in his *Memoirs of the Whig Party;* while his speech in support of Chatham's motion to stay hostilities in America was pronounced by the younger Pitt to have been "one of the most interesting and forcible that he had ever heard, or even could imagine." 4
Bentham rode and read with Lord Shelburne, or drew "little Henry" out in his coach—an attention for which he was wont to be rewarded by " a pair of the sweetest smiles imaginable from his mamma and his aunt." People here, he wrote to Wilson, do just what they please—eat their meals either with the family or in their own apartments. He was, indeed, never more at ease in his life, " one point excepted, the being obliged by *bien-siance* to dress twice a day." Forty years Letter to Sir James Macintosh (1808); Bow., x. p. 428. Romilly's *Memoirs,* i. p. 315.
Vol. i. p. 41; cited Fitzmaurice's *Shelburne,* ii. p. 325. *Chatham Correspondence,* vol. iv. p. 438; cited Fitzmaurice, iii. p. 9. Lord Henry Petty *(1780-1863),* the only son of Lord Shelburne's second wife; he became third Marquis of Lansdowne. The elder son of Lord Shelburne (Lord Fitzmaurice, afterwards Wycombe), then about fifteen, had, since he was six years old, been under the care of Mr. Jervis, a dissenting minister, and, for some time, also under the guidance of Dr. Priestley. Letter to his father, 31st August, 1781; Bow., x. p. 97. afterwards he described a curious scene, which occurred within a few days of his arrival at Bowood. Before supper was served for the rest of the company, he used to retire for the night, and, on the way to his chamber, had occasion to pass through a room containing a table whereon the guests deposited their bedroom lights. Repairing to this room one evening for his candles, he was in the act of taking them up when he was met by the master of the house, with the lights which he had come to place on the table. "'Mr. Bentham,' said he, candles in hand, 'Mr. Bentham,' in a tone somewhat hurried, as his manner sometimes was,' what is it you can do for me?' My surprise could not but be visible. Candle still in hand—' Nothing at all, my lord,' said I, 'nothing that I know of; I never said I could. I am like the Prophet Balaam: the word that God putteth into my mouth, that alone can I ever speak.' For discernment he was eminent; for quickness of perception not less so. He took this for what it was meant— a declaration of independence. He deposited his candles; I went off with mine. If by this rencontre any expectation of his was disappointed, neither his kindness nor the marks of his esteem were lessened.'" Bentham turned his dressing-room into a study; but he found little time for reading, and the progress of the Penal Code was deplorably slow. "I had just got into a mizmaze," said he; "I could not see my way clearly—it Bow., i. p. 249. According to Bowring, Bentham gave in conversation a different account of what was apparently the same interview. "Lord Shelburne asked me what *he* could do for *me.* I told him 'nothing'; and he found this so different to the universal spirit of those about him as to endear me to him. " (/., *x.* p. 116.) was a dark forest—for the vast field of law was around me with

all its labyrinths. Little by little great principles threw their light upon the field, and the path became clear." With the ladies of the house he was in great favour; they engaged him at chess and billiards, and shared his devotion to music. "After dinner, while the gentlemen are still at their bottle, I steal to the library, where I meet Lady Shelburne, and wait on her to her dressing-room; there"—he explained to his father, who was mightily pleased to hear of Jeremy amidst such distinguished surroundings— "we have music of some kind or other, unless there happen to be ladies in the house who are not musically disposed." When the gentlemen left the dining-room, or, if the weather were fine, had returned from a stroll in the grounds, the ladies and Bentham rejoined them in the library to drink coffee; after which, unless Lady Shelburne wanted him to make one at whist, it was absolutely necessary, he declared, that he should be in readiness to play at chess with Miss Fox, "whose Cavaliere Servente I have been ever since she came here from Warwick Castle in exchange for Miss Vernon."
Caroline Fox, daughter of Stephen second Lord Holland, who had married Lady Mary Fitzpatrick, was a niece of Lady Shelburne. In this same letter to his father she is described by Bentham as a "sprightly, good-natured little girl, not fourteen, but forward for Admission to her dressing-room on the ground floor was a mark of favour by which Lady Shelburne distinguished a "very few" among her many guests. Lord Shelburne kept a sort of open house and was frequently intruded on by somewhat unwelcome visitors. (Bow., x. p. 557.) E her age." She was born on the 3rd Nov., 1767, and lived until March, 1845. A crayon sketch of her was drawn by Lord Camden's daughter and presented to Bentham during his visit: she was, said he, prettily made, though her face was rather too long—and a Fox mouth, with a set of teeth white but too large, "saved her from being a beauty." It was Miss Fox for whom—as the child grew into a woman—Bentham conceived a deep and abiding affection; and with her and the other ladies of Bowood, under the designation of his guardian angels, he kept up a long and lively correspondence. "Favours like this," he said, replying to one of the Bowood letters, "are a bounty upon ill-humour. I must e'en pout on were it only in this view, as a froward child, that has been used to have its crying stopped by sugar-plums, keeps on roaring to get more of them. Query, what degree of perverseness would be sufficient to procure a sugar-plum from Miss Fox?"

Many years later he addressed to that lady a formal offer of marriage. This proposal—made in 1805, shortly after the renewal of a friendly intercourse which had been long interrupted—was rejected by Miss Fox in a gracious letter, professing profound respect and esteem for one whom she would ever gratefully remember, and begging him, without the waste of a single day, to return to those occupations from which the world would thereafter derive benefit and himself renown. "Health and success attend your labours, and if I must be remembered, let it be as one most sincerely interested in all the good that befalls you. So once again, God bless you—and farewell!" The refusal proved a bitter and lasting disappointment to Bentham, and it is related by Bowring that, a quarter of a century afterwards, not long before his death, he wrote a playful letter to the lady, speaking of the grey hairs of age and the bliss of youth, but the response was so cold and distant as to cause the old man much distress.

Bentham accompanied Lord Shelburne on a short visit to Lord Pembroke at Wilton, where they met young Beckford of Fonthill, the future author of *Vathek,* whose coming of age was just about to be celebrated by a grand fete. There, too, was Lord Bristol, Bishop of Derry, who afterwards joined the party at Bowood. The Bishop is described by Bentham as a most excellent and intelligent companion, who had been everywhere and knew everything: "He did not believe in revealed religion, was very tolerant in his judgment of others, and in political opinions most liberal. " The revenue of the Bishopric was *£7,200,* with the patronage of some forty advowsons, none of the livings being less than £250. Of the incumbents scarce one resided; they paid a curate £50 a year, which (as the Bishop observed to Bentham) was, according to their own estimation, what the service done was worth. The proper amount of emoluments which should attach to *any* office may be ascertained by a general method, simple as it is efficacious—wrote Bentham a few years later—Allow the official to discharge his duty by *'759-'44-Vathek* was written in French about 1782, and an English translation appeared in 1784. Beckford "played the harpsichord delightfully." *lyjo-iSoj.* A supporter of Parliamentary Reform and of Catholic Emancipation.
deputy, and mark what is paid to the deputy; the salary of the deputy is the proper salary for the place. Applying this rule to the emoluments of the clergy, the current price of curacies, where the curate takes the sole charge, affords *primd facie* a guide to the proper price which should be given for the services rendered. For ensuring the due performance of all the duties of the office, this price is found to be sufficient: "I say always *prima facie"* adds Bentham, " for, in reality, the current price is somewhat greater, part of the price being made up in hope."
Among other guests at Bowood were William Pitt (/75p-/?od), and his brother, Lord Chatham *17561835).* Pitt is described by Bentham as very goodnatured and a little raw, with nothing of the orator in his conversation: "I was monstrously frightened at him, but when I came to talk with him, he seemed frightened at me."

One day the pair rode out together and talked over Indian affairs. Pitt was "like a great school boy," scorning and sneering, and laughing at everything and everybody. He proposed a game of chess, but, being soundly beaten, complained that " it hurt his head," and would play no longer. Thereupon, Chatham, "who had Bow., ii. p. 242. Bentham also remarks on the *inequality* observable in the emoluments of the clergy; a reward so unequal degrades those who receive only their proper portion.

Pitt, the second (said Bentham more than forty years afterwards), had that quality—the only quality necessary for a Ministerial leader—the quality of an orator. He had no plans—good or bad—wide or narrow. In fact, he came into office too young to have any—just at the age when a man is entrusted with the conduct of his own private affairs. his father's Roman nose," gave Bentham a challenge, which was readily accepted. "From something that Pitt had said, I expected," wrote Bentham to George Wilson, "to have found him (Chatham) an easy conquest, especially as there was something seemingly irregular in the opening of his game; but it was a confounded bite, for I soon found his hand as heavy over me as I ever have felt yours; in short, he beat me shamefully, and the outcries I made on that occasion were such as would naturally convey to other people a formidable idea of his prowess."

Bentham had brought down to Bowood and given to his host a copy of the recently printed proofs of the proposed work on the Penal Code, which were not, as we have seen, published until 1789, when they appeared, with some additions, as *An introduction to the Principles of Morals and Legislation.* In spite of determined opposition from the author, Lord Shelburne persisted in reading this "driest of all dry metaphysics" to the ladies after tea, and, as Lord Camden and Dunning were expected to join the party, he pressed Bentham to prolong his stay at Bowood and submit his proof sheets to the two great lawyers.

Camden (1713-94), son of Sir John Pratt, Chief Justice of the King's Bench, had been successively Attorney-General, Chief Justice of the Common Pleas, and Lord Chancellor. He was a Whig, and, in the case of Wilkes, had pronounced boldly against the legality of "general" warrants, but he is represented, by Bentham, September 24th, 1781; Bow., x. p. 103.

Vide ante, p. 42.

as having an " undisguised aversion" from law reform in any shape whatsoever. In fluency and aptitude of diction he was, in Bentham's eyes, the equal of Mansfield, in argument perhaps his superior: "Not so in grace and dignity, in which two qualities neither recollection presents to view, nor is imagination equal to paint, anything superior to Mansfield."

The distinguished guests arrived in due course, but do not seem to have concerned themselves much with the author or his book. Lord Camden professed that he found a difficulty in understanding it, and Bentham, who, if not actually vain, was at all times absurdly sensitive, conceived, on somewhat shadowy grounds, the idea that neither Camden nor Dunning liked him. The Ex-Chancellor was, according to him, a hobbledehoy and had no polish of manners; from the very first, the tone of his address carried with it a sort of "coldness and reserve"—the future Lord Ashburton, though a most able advocate, was a narrow-minded man and a mere lawyer. Dunning was, indeed, a remarkable personage —of small stature, with limbs almost deformed, and disfigured by a short crooked nose; it is said, too, that his voice was bad, his utterance rapid and marked by a Devonshire accent, while his head shook as though with palsy—yet he possessed extraordinary power as an advocate and debater. Horne Tooke used to tell a story illustrative of his personal appearance: One evening Lord Thurlow went to the coffee-house which Dunning frequented and inquired for him; the waiter, being new to the place, did not know him, whereupon Thurlow, with an oath, cried: "Not know him! Go into the room upstairs, and, if you see any gentleman like the knave of clubs, say he is particularly wanted." It seems extremely doubtful whether the supposed "disgust" for Bentham was in fact entertained, either by Camden or Dunning, yet, nearly half a century afterwards, Bentham emphasised his belief in its existence, and was at pains to argue that there could surely have been no just cause for aversion, as the feeling was not shared either by Camden's daughter or by Dunning's wife.

"Enter, first, *Miss Pratt.* When upon my fiddle's overpowering her voice, the part of Hogarth's enraged musician was played by her noble and learned father, his rage was rendered the less distressing to me by his daughter's not appearing to be a sharer in it. Not that there was not war between us; not that she was not the aggressor; but, whatever was the cause of the war, it was anything but that. I remember not whether it was before or after this that a letter came to me, as from a gentleman, who had been of the company, alluding to offence received from me, and suggesting the propriety of a rencontre. The gentleman was a quiet gentleman, and nothing had passed between us. It was a forgery: the forger was discovered; it was Miss Pratt. Flagrant was the enormity. The investigation had not been indelicate. Vengeance would have been justice. But mediatrixes surrounded me. Mercy took the place of justice. The father was neither party nor privy. This was the first time of my seeing the lady; it was also the last. More than thirty years had elapsed, when the aunt of the late Marquis of Londonderry, being in Walker's *Original* (1835).

The incident is narrated, *post,* p. 63. The challenge ended: '' Swords or pistols, choose your weapons, as they are equal to your humble and offended servant, J. Brookes." (Bowring, x. p. 110.) company with a friend of mine, took notice of the pleasant days she had that year passed at Bowood. The adversary she had made to herself was not unremembered.

"At this time, or some subsequent one, I received in the bosom of the same family, a general invitation from her now noble brother, the present Marquis. Sensibility to the kindness was not wanting. But he had not been witness to anything of what had befallen on me from his father: without business or special invitation, I never went anywhere: and a house, in which the head is cold, is not a house to visit at. This last piece of evidence is upon my brief; but in a court of justice I should pause before I called the witness. The invitation was of the number of those which are not quite so likely to be remembered by the giver as by the receiver.

"Next comes *Mrs. Dunning.* Her husband, on his arrival at Bowood, found her there, and he left her there. Her stay was considerable—*her* voice, too, my fiddle had accompanied, as also her piano, on which she was a proficient. No complaint of overloudness there. The aversion, whatever it may be, that had been conceived by the husband—had it been shared in by the wife? About ten or eleven years had elapsed, when an incident occurred, which may be regarded perhaps as affording some proof of the negative.

"Lord Ashburton had paid the debt of nature. One day, at Lansdowne House, the master of it took me aside, and in express terms, after an eulogium pronounced on the dowager, gave it me as his opinion, that should my wishes point that way, disappointment was not much to be apprehended. The Miss (afterwards Lady Elizabeth) Pratt's brother was created Marquis of Camden in 1812.
Quare, see Bowring, x. p. 111. In 1781 Bentham wrote to G. Wilson: "She plays on the harpsichord most divinely. I have just been accompanying her." *(Ibid,* p. 107.) And again, in a letter to his father: "Mrs. Dunning is a perfect mistress of the harpsichord, and a very agreeable woman, though not very young nor handsome; but that's Mr. D. 's concern, not mine." *(Ibid,* p. 1ll.) case was sufficiently intelligible. The Lady's only son—the present Lord—was a minor, and in tender age. 'Your son,' said he, 'requires a guardian. Mr. Bentham would be a faithful one. Your brothers are engrossed by other cares.' No such conversation had indeed been mentioned to me; but circumstances sufficiently spoke it. My surprise was considerable; gratitude not inferior. But the offer was of the sort of those which may be received in any numbers, while at most only one at a time can be profited by. I have mentioned brothers. The founder of the *Baring* dynasty was one of them. He and I were good friends. Much of all this is but too little to the purpose. But what is to the purpose is—that, in a family, in which whatever is best in aristocratical manners was at the highest pitch of refinement, whatever aversion was entertained by the great Law Lords was peculiar to the confederacy, and was not shared in by those who, had any ordinary cause of disgust had place, would naturally have been most sensible to it.

The Historical Preface to the second edition of the *Fragment,* from which the foregoing extract is taken, though written, during the year 1822, in Bentham's later and somewhat difficult style, throws considerable light on the reception of the original issue of that work. It affords, moreover, an interesting glimpse of the author's relations with Lord Shelburne and his guests during this first memorable visit to Bowood: we, accordingly, extract, in an Appendix to this chapter, a few passages selected from the " Preface" (Bow., i. pp. 240-56).
Bentham asserted that Lord Shelburne had many projects for marrying him to ladies of his acquaintance. (Bow., x. p. 117; cf. *ib.,* p. 124.) Alexander Baring—son of Sir Francis, the founder of the house—was in 1835 created Lord Ashburton (the second creation). EXTRACTS FROM THE HISTORICAL PREFACE TO THE FRAGMENT ON GOVERNMENT.
"The first personage to be produced is Wedderburne; at the time here spoken of, Solicitor-General; afterwards, with the title of Lord Loughborough, Chief-Justice of the Common Pleas, and under that and the subsequent title of Earl of Rosselyn, Lord Chancellor.

"The Fragment had not been out long, when a *dictum* which it had drawn from him, showed me but too plainly the alarm and displeasure it had excited. The audacious work had come upon the carpet: in particular, the principle of utility which it so warmly advocates: this principle, and the argument in support of it, in opposition to the Whig-Lawyer fiction of the *original contract.* 'What say *you* to it?' said somebody, looking at Wedderburne. *"Answer.*—'It is a dangerous one.' This appalling word, with the application made of it to the principle, contains all that was reported to me. Of the rest of the conversation nothing; any more than of the other parties to it: for on this as on other similar occasions, what came to me came through cautious strainers: attached to me, more or less, by principle and affection, but to the adversary by pressing interests. The *dictum,* such as it is, though but from this one member of the conclave, will be a sufficient key to whatsoever might otherwise seem mysterious in the language or deportment of those others.
"Warm from the mouth of the oracle, the response was brought to me. What I saw but too clearly was—the alarm and displeasure of which it was the evidence: what I did not see was—the correct perception couched in it; the perception, I mean, of the tendency of the principle with reference to the Cf. *ante,* p. 41.
particular class, to the head of which the already elevated lawyer was on his way.

"Till within a few years—I am ashamed to think how few—did this same response remain a mystery to me. The principle of utility a dangerous principle! Dangerous, to endeavour to do what is most useful! The proposition (said I to myself) is a self-contradictory one. Confusion of ideas on his part (for I could find no other cause) was the cause to which I attributed it. The confusion was in mine. The man was a shrewd man, and knew well enough what he meant, though at that time I did not. By this time my readers, most of them, know, I hope, what he meant, as well as he. The paraphrase, by which upon occasion they would expound it, would be to some such effect as this:—' By *utility,* set up as the object of pursuit and standard of right and wrong in the practice of government, what this man means to direct people's eyes to is—that which, on each occasion, is most useful to all those individuals taken together, over whom Government is exercised. But to us, by whom the powers of Government are exercised over them,—to us, so far from being most useful, that which would be most useful to them, would, upon most occasions, be calamitous. Let this principle but prevail, it is all over with us. It is our interest, that the mass of power, wealth, and factitious dignity we enjoy at other people's expense, be as great as possible: it is theirs, that it be as small as possible. Judge, then, whether it is not dangerous to *us.* And who should *we* think of but ourselves?'

"Thus far Wedderburne. What this one lawyer said, all those others thought. And who knows how many hundred times they may not have said it?

"Not long after, I found myself in company with him. It was the first time and the only one. It was at the house of my intimate friend *Lind,* of whom presently. Any account given of me by him could not but have been in an eminent degree favourable. Wedderburne eyed me, but did not speak to me. He was still Solicitor-General. With all deference, I ventured some slight question to him. It was of a sort that any one could have put to any one. Answer short and icy.

"I come now to Lord Mansfleld. Not many days from the publication of the Fragment had elapsed, when he had not only taken cognisance of it, but been delighted by it. There was in those days a *Mr. Way,* who was, or had been, in office under him, and whom, it should seem, he had been in the habit of employing to read to him at odd times. Be this as it may, he was employed in reading this little work. Some connexions of mine were intimate with Mr. Way. The effects produced by it on the language and deportment of the noble and learned hearer were reported to them by this reader, and it may be imagined they were not long in reaching me. Some of the remarks that dropped from his Lord were also mentioned. While this or that passage was reading—' Now,' cried his Lordship, 'he seems to be slumbering:' while this or that other—' Now he is awake again.' Which were the sleepy parts, which the animated and animating ones, was at that time a mystery to me: to me it was at length cleared up: whether it be so to the reader, he will presently have to determine.

"This was not the only ground I had for expecting a favourable notice on the part of Lord Mansfield. On that occasion it had happened to me to minister, as will be seen presently, to an antipathy of his: on another occasion it fell in my way to minister to his self-complacency. I think, it was between A slightly different account is given by Bentham in a letter to Bowring, dated 30th January, 1827: "The deep bass voice & cold gravity of the crown lawyer still dwell on my ear & memory. Some little conversation with him fell to my share. " (Bow., x. p. 59.) Bentham says that there was "heart-burning" between the Chief Justice and his puisne Blackstone, who was glad "for quiet" to "slip down" into the Common Pleas. "To the Puisne, sitting on the same Bench with the scorning and overpowering Chief was sitting in hot water. 'I *have not been consulted and I will be heard,'* said another of his puisnes once in my hearing:—it was Willes, son to the Chief Justice." the publication of the Fragment on Government and that of the Introduction to Morals and Legislation that I took my second trip to Paris. In the passage boat from Dover I joined company with *David Martin.* David Martin was a Scotchman: he was a portrait painter; he had painted a portrait of Lord Mansfield; his errand to Paris was to procure an artist, to make an engraving of it. From an English hand, an engraving that would be satisfactory was not to be had for less than 1500 guineas. *Strange* (I remember his mentioning) was the artist, by whom the price had been required. The young painter's errand to Paris was to import a cheaper one. The expedition was not altogether fruitless. Two engravings there are, and I believe no more than two considerable ones, of Lord Mansfield. One represents him in the zenith of his political career; the other, near the close of it. The earliest is that for which his admirers are indebted to the brush, and in no small degree to the graver, of David Martin. While at Paris, Martin and I took up our quarters in the same lodging-house. His inquiries brought him to an engraver, whose name was *Littret de Montigny;* they entered into an agreement; I drew up the articles of it. The subject was not without its difficulties; the language French: I am but a sorry Frenchman now; I was, I imagine, not quite so bad an one then. My performance went through the hands of several Frenchmen, artists as well as others; one alteration alone being made in it; the substitution of the word *art* to the word *metier,* which, with unconsciously offensive impropriety, I had employed. The artist was imported; but perseverance failed: the task of finishing fell back into the hands of the painter, as above.

"Martin was familiar at Ken Wood. To the noble and learned patron, the Parisian expedition could not be an uninteresting one: particulars were called for and given:—the document was produced. He read it and took particular notice of it: it received his unqualified approbation. The draught was, in the whole complexion of it, one of the ordinary track of business. He inquired who the draughtsman was, and was informed.

"From the first morning on which I took my seat on one of the hired boards, that slid from under the officers' seats in the area of the King's Bench (it was about ten years before the publication of the Fragment), at the head of the gods of my idolatry had sitten the Lord Chief Justice. What his politics were, I did not comprehend; but, being his, they could not but be right. Days and weeks together have I made my morning pilgrimage to the chief seat of the living idol, with a devotion no less ardent and longing, and somewhat less irrational, than if it had been a dead one. Summons to the interior would have been admission into Paradise. No such beatification was I predestinated to receive. The notice taken of my Fragment had kindled my hopes; the notice taken of my draught had revived them; they were revived a second time, and with no better result.

"Now as to Lord Camden. The preparatory mention of Lord Shelburne was necessary to the mention of his political associates and advisers, and in particular this their Chief. I was already at Bowood, when the ex-Chancellor, with his unmarried daughter, made their appearance. The marked kindness and attention shown to me in that family could leave no doubts as to the manner in which I had been spoken of to the grave personage. From the very first, however, the manner of his address to me carried with it in my eyes a sort of coldness and reserve. This being the first time of my seeing him,—I was not in a condition to form an immediate judgment, whether such was his general manner, or whether there was anything in it, that applied in a particular manner to myself.

According to Shelburne, Lord Camden always said that he was sure Lord Mansfield never decided a cause right or wrong from a pure motive all his life! (Fitzmaurice's *Life of Shelburne,* i. p. go.)

"Of the drift of my book, and the sort of sensation it had made, it is not in the nature of the case he should have been ignorant: not a syllable on the subject did he ever say to me. He saw the countenance that was shown to me by every body else: no such countenance did *he* ever show to me. No advance did I ever make to him: to him, in his situation, it belonged, not to me, in mine, to make advances. On no occasion did he ever make any to me.

"Not many days had elapsed, when a little incident helped to strengthen my suspicions. One evening after dinner, Miss Pratt was singing: I was accompanying her on the violin. 'Not so loud! Not so loud! Mr. Bentham!' cried Lord Camden, tone and manner but too plainly indicating displeasure.

"' You eat too much, Mr. Bentham!' said he one day to me; nor was there any want of hearers. 'You eat too much. Reading so much as you do, two or three ounces a day should be enough for you.' The fact was—all the rest of the company sat down to two meals of meat: I, unless when forced, never to more than one. At that one, if excess was ever observed, none was ever experienced. Two purposes seemed as if aimed at: representing me as a glutton, and representing me as that sort of bookworm, by which nothing could ever be *'done for'* his noble friend. In a similar strain was what little he ever said to me. 'But your own deportment:' says some body—' may there not have been something in it that was displeasing to him?' To this point I shall speak presently.

"A man of such celebrity, and who had for so many years occupied the first places in the law, could not fail of awakening, in a man in my situation and of my turn of mind, a desire to form some conception of the bent of *his.* I observed his In a letter written at the time to G. Wilson (2nd October, 1781), Bentham describes Miss Pratt as "a charming girl in every respect but beauty." (Bow., x. p. 113.) conversation; I observed the books he opened, and set before him. I watched with particular interest every opportunity of observing, whether the system of law ever presented itself to his mind, as being, in any part of it, or as to any point in it, susceptible of melioration. By nothing I could ever catch, could I ever divine that any such conception had ever entered into his head:—with the exception of here and there an anecdote, such as the sphere he had always moved in could not fail to have furnished him with, I heard nothing in his talk that might not have been heard in any drawing-room, or in any coffeehouse.

"I come now to John Dunnlng.

"It was one evening after dinner that he made his appearance. He came fresh from Bristol, of which city he was Recorder. I found him standing in a small circle, recounting his exploits. They were such as, when associated with the manner in which he spoke of them, and the feelings that sat on his countenance, brought up to me Lord Chief-Justice Jefferies. He had been the death of two human beings: he looked and spoke as if regretting there had not been two thousand. Upon my approach, the scowl that sat on his brow seemed more savage than before. The cause I had not at the time any suspicion of: the effect was but too visible. As I came up, he was wiping his face: the weather was warm, and he had in various ways been heated. It was the tail only of a sentence that I heard. It appeared to me incorrect: I expressed a hope that it was so. Subdued and respectful (I well remember) was my tone; for, notwithstanding the freedom to which no member of the Bar could have been unaccustomed,—the temerity, such as it was, was by no means unaccompanied with the fear of giving offence. The scowl was deeper still: he Lord Camden told Lord Lansdowne that he found a difficulty in understanding the Introduction to the *Principles of Morals and Legislation',* and that, therefore, others would. (Bow. , x. p. 185.) *Vide ante,* pp. 42, 54. made no answer: he took no further notice of me: bystanders smothered a titter as well as they could. Supper was soon after served: it was a meal of which I never partook. He went off the next morning: I saw no more of him: I had seen quite as much as was agreeable to me.

"In conversation with Lord Shelburne once, an observation of mine was—that what Junius says of the practice of the long robe, when he calls it 'the indiscriminate defence of Right and *Wrong,'* is not precisely true; for that, upon the whole, *Wrong,* in his quality of best customer, enjoys a pretty decided preference. 'Natural enough,' replied my noble friend: and I remembered hearing it observed of Dunning, that he never seemed to do the thing so much *con amore,* as when the wrong was on his side.

"Last comes Colonel Barre.

"On his arrival at Bowood, he too found me already established there: Barre" was a perfect man of the world. Dunning was sitting for one of Lord Shelburne's seats: Barre for another. Speeches are assigned to him in the Debates, and mention is made of him in Junius:—similes are there described to Mr. Burke:' sarcasms to 'Colonel Barre. ' But In a letter written at the time (October, 1781), Bentham gave a very different account of this incident: "With Dunning I could have no communication; there was no time for it, except a joke or two, which the devil tempted me to crack upon him, immediately upon his coming in." (Bowring, x. p. 113.)

'Born 1726. Served with distinction under Wolfe on the coast of France, where he became acquainted with Shelburne, then Lord Fitzmaurice. (Fitzmaurice's *Life ofShelburru,* i. p. 118.) Writing to G. Wilson, 19th September, 1781, Bentham said: "Barri loves to sit over his claret, pushes it about pretty briskly, and abounds in stories that are well told and very entertaining. He really seems to have a great command of language; he states clearly & forcibly; and, upon all points his words are fluent & well chosen." (Bowring, x. p. 104.) In 1790 Bentham wrote: "Barrel though he knew nothing, was a good party bull dog, barked well, and with great imposition and effect, where nothing was necessary to be known." *(Ibid.,* p. 236). F his great merit was martyrdom: he had suffered under the third of the Georges, as of late Sir Robert Wilson under the fourth. Being a soldier of fortune, he was regarded as being, in a more exclusive degree, the property of his patron. When the patron became Minister, an indemnity, value 3000 a-year, was given to the *protegi* During his ministry, the patron occupied the villa at Streatham, at which Brewer Thrale used to entertain Burke, Johnson, and their associates. I was sitting there after dinner with Lord Shelburne and Barre',— no one else present but Lady Shelburne,—when the print was brought in, which represents Lord Shelburne giving the dole to Barrd in the character of *Belisarius:* both are striking likenesses.

"Now as to what passed at Bowood between him and me. Towards others, his deportment was easy: towards myself, stately, distant, and significant. What (said I to myself) can I do to propitiate this minor divinity? Except from the sort of reports that give nothing but the surface, he was altogether unknown to me. In my portmanteau I had imported two articles:—an unfinished quarto in print, of which presently,— and a manuscript of between a dozen and a score of pages. It was an attack upon *Dcodands.* When a man, who has a child and a waggon, loses the child by the waggon's going over it,— a notion, that my paper has been labouring to produce, was— that the loss of the child would be suffering enough, without the loss of the waggon's being added to it. Different has been, and continues to be, the opinion of the sages of the law; so, of course, of those who worship them. —'English' are all our institutions: this, as well as every other.

"The Colonel being a soldier, not a lawyer, while presenting him with this specimen of them, little did I think of encountering in his mind any very formidable prepossession. Vain confidence!

Walpole describes Barr£ as the bravo selected by Shelburne to run down Pitt. (Fitzmaurice's *Life of Shelburne,* i. p. 125.)

"One day, finding him alone at the common reading-table, I put into his hand my little paper. A day or two after, I ventured to ask whether it had been looked at. 'Mr. Bentham,' said he, returning it with a look and tone of scorn, *'you have got into a scrape.'*

" Scrape, Colonel! what scrape? I know of no scrape the case admits of.' No answer. The unfortunate paper was pocketed. I went my way, and there the matter ended.

"' You are a greenhorn: you know nothing of the world. You wrote that book of yours; you made your foolish attacks upon the lawyers; you thought it would be a treat to us to see you running at them: you are a silly fellow; you don't know how necessary they are to us. What have we to do with the *Deodands t* you thought to cut a figure; you have *got yourself into a scrape.'* In this paraphrase, I found the interpretation— the only one I could ever find—for the appalling riddle. A confirmation, which this interpretation received, will be seen presently. It was not, however, received till some years afterwards.

"Meantime, a little incident rendered me a little more fortunate: it recovered for me more or less of the ground which the Deodand had lost me. It was at the dawn of the French Revolution. Some of the leading men were in London. The Lansdowne House cook not being yet arrived from the country (it was the autumn of 1788), the dinner was given at Colonel Barre's. Circumstances were such, that I could not well have been left out of the invitation. In the drawing room the conversation turned upon the House of Commons' debates. The Colonel's name had been looked for and not found. The remark touched upon a sore place—so I found afterwards. Embarrassment was visible. I stept in to his relief. '*M. le Colonel* said I, '*est comme le Dieu dans la fable: il ne paroit que dans les grandes occasions'* A buzz of applause ran round: the Colonel, whom / had got out of *this scrape,* was most conspicuous and most audible.

"It was two or three years after this that the enigma of the *scrape* received the solution above hinted at. When my proposal, for a Penitentiary System upon the *Panopticon* plan, had received acceptance, Colonel Barre, with every body else, knew of it.

"Speaking to a common friend who had been acting officially on the occasion of it,—' I am glad,' said he, 'to see Mr. Bentham turning his hand to useful things.' Seeing that I do not betray his name, the friend, whether he remembers it or no, will, I hope, pardon me. Why was the one thing *useful,* while the other was so much otherwise as to have got me into a *scrape?* The reader has, perhaps, already answered for me. Neither the lawyer tribe, nor any other section of the ruling few, had any *visible* interest in the evils to which the Panopticon plan would have applied a remedy. A prison, in which all the prisoners could, at all times, be seen at a glance by the keeper,—without his being seen by any of them, or changing his place,—was more intelligible than a *Deodand:* and, if a man, who had then the whole Ministry with him— Pitt, Dundas, Rose, every body—could be said to be in a *scrape,* it could not be a very pitiable one.

"I have mentioned the Colonel's embarrassment. The cause of it was this; I knew it not till afterwards. Person and manner imposing; self-possession perfect. But ignorance was extraordinary;

extraordinary even in Honourable House: indolence not less so. From Dunning, the patron used to extract his information; to Barre, he was forced to administer it. 'The trouble I used to have in fighting him up' (that was Lord Shelburne's expression to me one day)' is altogether inconceivable.'

"The inaptitude of the showy soldier may perhaps furnish an additional means of interpretation for the ' *What-can-you do-for-me f'" (vide ante,* p. 48). Sir Evan Nepean, successively Under-Secretary of State, and Secretary to the Admiralty: he died in 1822, as the "Preface" was passing through the press.

"A natural enough object of curiosity will be the sort of sensation produced by the little work, in the mind of the learned Author, whose great work is the subject of it. Some small satisfaction, on this point likewise, it happens to be in my power to afford. It had not long been out, when from one quarter or another, the intelligence was brought to me. The question had been asked him—I never knew from whom—for in telling such tales out of school great caution was in every instance observed: be this as it may, a question had been asked him—whether he knew who the Author was?' No, was the answer; 'not his name: all I know of him is where he comes from:—he is a Scotchman.' The conjecture had much better grounds than those others that have been mentioned. The Scotch minds were less ill-suited than the English to the sort of business he saw done. The Scotch law having for its foundation the Roman,—the range of thought, in the field of law, is necessarily much less narrow, among Scotch than among English lawyers. By the arguments in the Fragment, their sinister interests, their interest begotten prejudices, their reputation, are not so directly struck at, as those of their southern brethren. As to *fiction,* in particular, compared with the work done by it in English law, the use made of it in theirs is next to nothing. No need have they had of any such clumsy instruments. They have two others, and of their own making, by which things of the same sort have been done with much less trouble. *Nobite officium* gives them the creative power of legislation: this, and the word *desuetude* together the annihilative. Having less need of insincerity than the English,—language has with them been less impudently insincere. When the English said King James the second had *abdicated* his throne,—the contrary being true in the eyes of every body,—the Scotch said he had *forfeited* it. So much as to intrinsic evidence.

"Now as to extrinsic. By the sort of notices taken of the The *Fragment on Government; vide ante,* p. 35.

Fragment by Lord Mansfield, as above, a suspicion might naturally enough be produced in the mind of the harassed Puisne, that the adversary was a sort of sad dog, of the Scotch breed, set upon him by the overbearing Chief.

"A question somebody else put to the Author of the Commentaries was—whether it was his intention to make any answer to the critique?' No,' was the reply; not even if it had been better written.' But, though he made not any answer to it, nor any express mention of it by its name, he did not altogether refrain from noticing it. In the preface to the then next edition of his work, (and, I take it for granted, to all subsequent ones) there are allusions to it Intimation is given, that the work would be the better, instead of the worse, for the attack thus made on it. So far as regarded the currency of his work,—if ever I entertained expectations of seeing it lessened, as for aught I know I did, they were pretty effectually disappointed. What, at that time, I had not sufficiently perceived was—that, for the sort of work that *his* is, the demand was in its nature boundless: for the sort of work that mine was, the demand is bounded by very narrow limits. What the law is, or is likely to be taken to be,—every man, if it were possible, and not too much trouble to him, would know. What the law ought to be, is as yet of the number of those things, about which few indeed,—on any points, except such few and comparatively narrow ones, in which it has happened to a man to take some particular interest,—either know any thing or care.

"We never met: two years, however, had not elapsed, before we were on better terms. The Penitentiary System had for its first patrons Mr. Eden (the Mr. Eden above spoken of) and Sir William Blackstone. They framed in conjunction— and without exposure to sale, circulated—the draught of a Bill for that purpose. A copy (I do not remember how) found its way into my hands. Some friend of mine (I think) gave it me, *i.e.* Blackstone; see *ante,* p. 60, note ().
without saying how he had come by it. It gave rise on my part to my second work, entitled, *A View of the Hard Labour Bill,* written and published in 1778. A copy of it, communicated, as far as I remember, in the same way, went to Mr. Eden, and another to Mr. Justice Blackstone. In the mode of communication, I followed the example that had been set me. The tone of this second comment, though free, and holding up to view numerous imperfections, was upon the whole laudatory: for my delight at seeing symptoms of ever so little a disposition to improvement, where none at all was to be expected, was sincere, and warmly expressed. From Mr. Eden, the communication produced an answer of some length; cold, formal, distant and guarded; written, as a man writes, when he feels what he is not willing to acknowledge: no desire expressed of any verbal communication. He was then on the eve of his departure for the now United States, with Governor Johnstone, and I forget who else, with proper chains in their hands:—chains which the refractory Americans were to be invited to put upon their necks. Between twenty and thirty years after, the earliest of the works edited by M. Dumont having come out, I had the pleasure of numbering a nephew of his Lordship's, Sir Frederick Eden, among my declared disciples, and not many years ago the pain of losing in him a highly valued friend.

"From the Judge I received a note, which still exists, I believe, somewhere: of every thing that is material in the terms of it, I have pre,erved the memory. After thanks, and so forth, in the third person,—' some of the observations,' said he, 'he believed had already occurred to the framers of the Bill' (not mentioning himself as one of them), 'and many others were well deserving of their attention.' To any reader of this work, if any such there be by whom that other of mine has been perused, the frigid caution with which the acknowledgment is thus guarded—the frigid caution so characteristic of the person as well as the situation, will not have been unexpected.

"That the Fragment was not unknown to either of them, may readily be imagined: if so, to no man who has read it, will there be any thing wonderful in their reserve.

"To all this correspondence, George Wilson was of course privy; 'Bentham,' said he to me one day, 'don't you feel now and then some compunction, at the thought of the treatment your Fragment gives to Blackstone? Of all the men that ever sat on a Westminster Hall Bench, he is perhaps the only one that ever attempted any thing that had the good of the people, or the improvement of the law, for its object, independently of professional interest and party politics: think of the treatment he has received from you.' I did think of it:—and, had any good come of it in this instance, the more I had thought of it, with the greater satisfaction should I have thought of it. Little did I think—little, I am persuaded, did even he think—that, after the improvements made afterwards in the system—and by the universal opinion of that time they were no slight ones—it would have terminated in an hermetically-sealed Bastile, in which, at an expense to the public of 1ooo a-head for lodging alone, no more than six hundred will be provided for when the number is completed, instead of two thousand at no more than *£15* a-head; annual expense between 30 and *£40* a-year per head, instead of *£12,* which, upon the death of the first contractor, would have ceased. Such at least has been the computation made by an intelligent and honest hand.

"Be this as it may, was it for the Author of the Fragment to see cause of compunction in the effect thus produced in the case of Blackstone? No: unless it be for Bell and Lancaster to feel compunction for whatever good has been done by *'Excellent Church'* and her associates, towards the instruction of the people. In what instance, by any supporters of *'Matchless Constitution?* has this or any thing else been done, with any the least tinge of good in it, but with the feelings with which the ancient Pistol ate the leek, and the hope of defeating or obstructing something better?

"' Such being the tendency, such even the effects of the work, what became of it? how happened it, that, till now, not so much as a second edition had been made of it?' Questions natural enough; and satisfaction, such as can be, shall accordingly be given: words as few as possible.

"Advertisements, none. Bookseller did not, Author could not, afford any. Ireland pirated. Concealment had been the plan:—how advantageous, has been already visible. Promise of secrecy had accordingly been exacted: parental weakness broke it. No longer a great man, the Author was now a nobody. In catalogues, the name of Lind has been seen given to him. On the part of the men of politics, and in particular the men of law on all sides, whether endeavour was wanting to suppression may be imagined." CHAPTER IV RESIDENCE IN RUSSIA AND RELATIONS WITH DUMONT

AFTER leaving Bowood, in the autumn of 1781, 1. Bentham occupied himself with the preparation of a series of essays on Indirect Legislation and the Transplantation of Laws—years afterwards the manuscripts were handed to the author's Swiss friend and collaborator, Etienne Dumont (1759-1829), who made use of them in the *Trait/s de Legislation,* published at Paris in 1802. About the same time (in 1783) he published a translation of a work on chemistry written by one Bergman, a German, entitled, *An Essay on the Usefulness of Chemistry.* The translation appears to have been based on a French version, and not on the original German text.

Meanwhile, on the death of Rockingham in July, 1782, Shelburne had become Prime Minister, with Pitt as Chancellor of the Exchequer and Leader of the House of Commons. The new Premier could hardly See *Des Moyens indirect: de privenir des Dilits,* voL Hi. p. I; and *De t'Influence des Terns et des Lieux en matiire de Legislation, ibid.*, p. 325. For English versions, see Bow., i. pp. 533-580 and 169-194.
HaL, i. p. 296. be said to be attached to any party in politics; he has been variously described as the chief of the Chatham Whigs and as a Tory democrat; he supported the claims of the American colonists, yet spoke the language of a Friend of the King, of a defender of the prerogative, and declared that England ought not to be governed by a party or faction, that the Sovereign ought not to be *" un roi faineant"* A few years later he stoutly espoused the cause of Warren Hastings.
He had, according to Bentham, a following which by mere weight of reputation told in the balance against the great aristocracy, but "it was then, as they say at cricket, Shelburne against all England." Having, indeed, quarrelled with many of the great Whig families, he sought to rise by means of the people; "he was really radically disposed," said Bentham, "and witnessed the French Revolution with sincere delight."

His administration was shortlived, and the Premier, deserted by his old colleagues, gave place to a coalition Ministry, which took office for a few months under Portland. In 1784 Pitt, having come into power, secured a large majority at the polls, and, at his instance, Shelburne was created Marquis of Lansdowne.

Shortly after these events Bentham made preparation for a lengthy absence from England; he had long contemplated a visit to Russia, where his brother dwelt on an estate of Prince Potemkin,4 situate near Crichoff, a small town lying on the right bank of the river Don. Colonel Bentham was employed in the service of the Hal., i. p. 272. Bow., x. p. 236.

'*Ibid.*, p. 187. Prime Minister of Russia under Catharine II. Prince, and presided over an establishment designed to promote the introduction of various arts of civilisation into a barbarous region; the Colonel had a battalion of a thousand men under his command and was engaged as a Jack-of-all-Trades—" building ships, like Harlequin, of odds and ends, a ropemaker, a sailmaker, a distiller, brewer, maltster, tanner, glassman, glass-grinder, potter, hempspinner, smith, coppersmith." This experiment, in the end, proved a failure, and the Prince, after incurring a loss of many thousand pounds, sold the place to a Pole.

With a view to his intended visit, Bentham had begun, in the early part of 1785, to collect information on agricultural, trading, and manufacturing subjects; his anxiety to promulgate a " Code" led him, moreover, to think of enlisting the sympathy of Catharine of Russia in his codification project. Indeed, as early as 1779 he had written to his brother urging him to seek an opportunity of communicating his ideas to the Empress. "*Plutdt que de la manquer,"* he wrote, " *tu la guetteras dans les rues, tu te prosterneras devant elle, et aprds avoir mange' autant de poussiere que t & as envie, tu lui jetteras mon billet au nez, ou bien d la gorge, si elle veut bien que tes mains soient Id."* Written law, said Bentham, is the only law which merits the name of law; and it must be not only written, but also clear and systematic. Codification, to use the term coined by himself, was therefore essential. The sovereign, it is Letter 28th December, 1779; Add. MSS., Brit. Mus., 33,538, f. 423; cited Hal., i. pp. 153, 331. The original is in French. *Traitit de Ugisiation,* i. pp. 356, 365, 366.
true, cannot undertake the task of codification—entangled in the labyrinths of jurisprudence, a Caesar, a Charlemagne, a Frederick, would have been no more than an ordinary man. But suppose a perfect code framed, the sovereign who should recognise its merit and give it support, would, so Bentham maintained, rank above all other sovereigns.
In August, 1785, he set out for Russia with valuable letters of introduction from Lord Lansdowne, who begged to assure him that he left the shores of England with the affectionate good wishes of every member of the Bowood circle. "I do assure you," he wrote, " that we are all (Miss Fox included, who is sitting by me) concerned for your going, independent of the loss of your company, which we always have considered as a resource when the interested and the factious deserted us." The writer forwarded an English sword to be conveyed as a present to Samuel Bentham, "the Russian Colonel," and enjoined his correspondent, with perhaps more prudence than propriety, to pass it for his own "to avoid the custom houses."

The route chosen was by way of Paris, Lyons, Nice, and Genoa to Smyrna, where the traveller stayed a month; but in no part of the tour does he appear to have made much use of the opportunities afforded by the introductions carried with him—"a strong curiosity," says Dr. Bowring, "was tempered and controlled by an unusual bashfulness."

Leaving Smyrna for Constantinople, Bentham embarked in a small heavily laden Turkish boat, which was *TraiUs de Legislation,* iii. p. 286. Bow., x. p. 148.
like to have foundered. One night, so great was the peril, he was summoned to leave his bed. Reflecting, however, that nothing he could do would be of any use, and that, if he was to be drowned, it would be best to be drowned asleep, he turned over and "slept as soundly that night as on any night before or after."

After touching at Scio and being driven by contrary winds into the harbour of Mitylene, he quitted this perfidious bark for a British vessel, in which he reached Constantinople about November. There he remained some five or six weeks with an English merchant, as no lodging-house accommodation could be procured. The ambassador, whom he found "full of friendship and politeness," would have received him in the Palace, but it was already occupied by a number of guests, including a certain Hon. Mr. Cadogan, on his way to Egypt, who, for the purpose of the expedition (so Bentham wrote to Lord Lansdowne) "was nourishing a pair of whiskers, which, respectable as they are from an Asiatic point of view, form an odd mixture with a garb in other respects completely English." From Constantinople the journey was made by land, and at Bucharest the traveller came across a Greek, who proved to be as great an admirer of Helvetius as he was himself—a circumstance noted with considerable relish.

In February, 1786, Bentham arrived at his brother's residence near Crichoff in White Russia, where for nearly two years he lived a secluded life, engaged for the most part in literary studies. He acquired some slight knowledge of the Russian language, enough to make November 14th, 1785; Bow., x. p. 157.
himself understood, though not enough to enable him to understand what was said to him. "I know just as much of Russ,"he used to say in later years, "as I know of the language of cats—I could speak their language and obtain an answer, but the answer I never understood. '.'

During his sojourn in Russia, he busied himself in the preparation of certain portions of the projected Penal Code in the French tongue—a course upon which his brother had always insisted as one calculated to render the work accessible to a much wider circle of readers, and so greatly enlarge its influence. Thus, in February, 1787, we find him writing to Wilson: "I am marginalcontenting *Essai sur les R/compenses,* about the size of Beccaria's Book, with Voltaire's comment added to it. It was begun to serve as one of the divisions of my great French work; but I found it detachable, so I swelled it out a little, and send it to you to do what you will with." He goes on to beg Wilson to find some Frenchman capable of revising and correcting the text, but the Essay was not, in fact, published for many years —it ultimately formed part of *Th/orie des Femes et des Recompenses* edited by Dumont, and published in 1811. I never saw an English translation that I could bear to read—he wrote to the Abbe

Morellet—and it was this consideration that set me upon writing such piles of barbarous French, as I have written to my great sorrow.

About the same time a rumour reached him that *i.e.* running an abridgement along the margin.
Crimes and Punishments (1764). Bow., x. p. 198.
Pitt contemplated a reduction of the rate of interest from five to four per cent. The news aroused his curiosity, and he sought confirmation from Wilson: "Tell me what you hear about it; were it true I should like to give him a piece of my mind. I have arguments against it ready *cut* and *dry*—the former epithet you may have some doubt about, the latter you will not dispute. You know it is an old maxim of mine that interest, as love and religion, and so many other pretty things, should be free." In ancient times *every* loan at interest was regarded as the extortion of unlawful gain, and as such adjudged to be against Scripture and the common law of England; indeed, if a man, *even after his death,* were found to be "an usurer," all his goods and chattels were forfeited to the king. But, for some centuries, the acceptance of interest at prescribed rates had been recognised by the legislature; and only such contracts or assurances as secured a profit beyond that allowed by positive law were avoided as usurious. By a statute of the reign of Queen Anne the rate had at length been reduced to five per cent., which was then, and long afterwards remained, the extremity of legal interest that could be taken for an ordinary loan of money.

The rumour as to Pitt's intentions was discredited; but Bentham, nevertheless, seized this opportunity of denouncing the prohibitory laws and, also, of discussing Adam Smith's references to the subject in the *Wealth of Nations*—a work, said he, which will rise in public estimation in proportion as genius shall be held in honour. He espied, lurking among the " precious and December, 1786; Bow., *x.* p. 167.
irrefragable" truths unfolded in that famous book, a notable fallacy, for the great economist was found to approve the five per cent, limitation. If, argued Dr. Smith, the restriction were removed, such loanable capital as is now available for "sober" people would be appropriated by reckless "prodigals," or by "projectors" seeking funds for the promotion of rash enterprises. No, urged Bentham, it is not only *prodigals* to whom money would be lent at extraordinary interest. Friends would either not lend at all or would lend at the ordinary rate, while strangers would only lend upon *security* if the borrower were not engaged in industry. But he who has security to offer, present or future, certain or contingent, need not pay at a higher rate merely because he is a prodigal. The same reasoning will not, it is true, apply to *projectors,* but the censure which condemned them would fall, so Bentham declared, upon every species of new industry; the odious name of "projects" being applied to the most useful enterprises. Now, even if it were proved that ruin attended every projector who engaged in a new branch of industry, it would not be just to conclude that the spirit of invention and enterprise ought to be discouraged. Though the original author of an invention may be ruined in his efforts to bring the discovery to perfection, yet out of the embers of failure success may arise and crown his labours. So soon as a new dye, more brilliant or more durable than the old ones, a new and more convenient machine, or a new and more profitable practice in agriculture has been discovered, a thousand dyers, ten thousand mechanicians, a hundred thousand 'o agriculturists may reap the benefit. Why, Adam Smith himself admits that certain "projects," even under the name of "dangerous and expensive experiments," should be encouraged by the grant of temporary monopolies!
In May, 1787, the manuscript of this renowned *Defence of Usury* was despatched to Wilson, and in the same year sent to the press by Jeremiah Bentham, who apparently took the step contrary to Wilson's wishes and advice. In this instance, at any rate, the intervention of the old man was certainly justified by the event, and that right speedily. The *Monthly Review* for May, 1788, spoke of the book as "a gem of the finest water," while Adam Smith pronounced it to be the work of a superior man, adding that he thought the author was in the right. "He has given me some hard knocks," Dr. Smith is reported to have said; "but in so handsome a manner that I cannot complain "; and, with the tidings of the doctor's death, Bentham received a copy of his works, which had been sent as a token of esteem. The glowing tribute of J. S. Mill is widely known, but, bestowed by so great an authority, it may well be here recalled. A statutory restriction on interest, said Mill, though approved by Adam Smith, has been condemned by all enlightened persons "since the triumphant onslaught made upon it by Bentham in his letters The title is: *"Defence of Usury,* showing the impolicy of the present legal restraints on the terms of pecuniary bargains; in a series of letters to a friend; to which is added a letter to Adam Smith, Esq., Ll.d., on the discouragements opposed by the above restraints to the progress of inventive industry." It was translated into French in 1790, and in the same year a second edition was called for. (See Bow., iii. pp. 1-29; and *Manual of Political Economy, ibid.,* p. 47.) on Usury, which may still be referred to as the best extant writing on the subject." These letters, remarks Lecky, gave what will probably prove a deathblow to a legislative folly that had been in existence for three thousand years. The doctrine that "all money is sterile by nature" is, he declared, an absurdity of Aristotle: "It is enough to make one ashamed of one's species to think that Bentham was the first to bring into notice the simple consideration that if the borrower employs the borrowed money in buying bulls and cows, and if these produce calves to ten times the value of the interest, the money borrowed can scarcely be said to be sterile or the borrower a loser." It has, too, been noted by Sir Leslie Stephen that Bentham's contemporary, Dugald Stewart, who almost ignores Bentham in his argument against Utilitarianism, throughout his lectures on Political Economy makes frequent and approv-

ing references to the tract on Usury.

On the appearance of a later edition in 1816, the *Edinburgh Review* spoke of it as that " inimitable performance" of Mr. Bentham, " to whom is due the rare praise of having at once begun and finished the task of opening men's eyes upon this subject"; and, in striking proof of the slowness with which reason acts as a solvent on English prejudices, the same Review, in 1828, referred to the fact that the Usury Laws were still in *Political Economy,* book v. chap. x. § 2. *Rationalism in Europe,* 4th ed., vol. ii. p. 260; cf. Stephen's *History of Criminal Law,* iii. p. 195. *Utilitarians,* vol. i. p. 160. *Edinburgh Review,* vol. xxvi. p. 271, and see vol. xxvii. p. 339. existence — although more than half a century had elapsed since the publication of Bentham's " unanswered and unanswerable essay, not less admirably reasoned than happily expressed."

It was during the visit to Crichoff that Bentham, with the aid of his brother, matured the ill-starred "Panopticon," or " Inspection House" plan, devised to carry into execution certain admirable principles of penal discipline, which had been conceived and developed under the influence of John Howard's book on the *State of Prisons?* Howard's publications, said he, afford a rich fund of materials; but a quarry is not a house: rules or hints for rules, recommendations of which the reason is not always apparent, but no leading principles, no order. My venerable friend, he continued, was more usefully employed than in arranging words and sentences: his kingdom was of a better world— the labours of the legislator or the writer are as far below his as earth is below heaven.

The fundamental conception of Bentham's plan was to construct a gaol such that all its parts should be visible from a single point by means of a series of reflectors; that is to say, a prison in which an inspector would be able to see at a glance everything that was taking place, the inspector being himself concealed from the observation of the prisoners, so as to beget "the *E.J?.,vo.* xlviii. p. 459. The Usury Laws were not abolished until 1854; as to "harsh and unconscionable" transactions, see 63 & 64 Vict. c. 51.

Published in 1777. Howard is referred to by Lecky as "that great Dissenter who, having travelled over 40,000 miles in works of mercy, at last died on a foreign soil a martyr to his cause." *History of Rationalism,* 4th ed., i. p. 347.) Bow. , iv. p. 121. sentiment of an invisible omniscience." To this architectural conception of central inspection Bentham added a proposal for *contract-management* (or, administration by *contract* as distinguished from *trust* management), based on a theory known in his compendious jargon as the *interest-and-duty-junction-prescribing* principle: *l'inte'rit p/cuniaire ne s'endort jamais.* The principle had been recognised in the Bill of 1778, and Bentham supplemented the original scheme by suggesting an arrangement analogous to that of life-assurance, whereby the director would have a pecuniary interest in lowering the average rate of mortality.

To the promotion of these projects for Prison Reform Bentham devoted many years of his life, and practically the whole of his fortune, elaborating the plan with every proposed detail of construction and every particular of the suggested methods of control.

Wilson received from Russia a pamphlet on Prison Discipline, but, regarding it as "small game," he declared the subject to be unpopular, and refused to send the manuscript to the press. A few years later—in 1791—a memoir on the plan was despatched by its author to M. Garran de Coulon, member of the Legislative Assembly and of a Committee for the Reform of Criminal Law. "Allow me to construct a prison on this model," said Bentham; "I will be the gaoler. You will see by the memoir that the gaoler will have no salary—will cost nothing to the nation." The Assembly ordered the memoir to be printed, but the state of *Traitls de Legislation,* iii. p. 229; Hal., i. p. 151.

19 Geo. 3, c 74, s. 18; *ante,* p. 38.

Bow., x. p. 269.

public affairs did not permit of any further steps being taken. Dr. Parr, who was described by Romilly as Bentham's "profound admirer and universal panegyrist," endeavoured to interest Charles Fox in the plan and its author; and in a letter to Bentham, in 1803, Romilly writes: "The first thing he (Dr. Parr) said to me the other day, when I met him in the street, was that he hoped I was a 'Panoptician.'" Pitt, too, gave the project favourable consideration, came in person to Bentham's house to examine the models, and, indeed, determined to secure for his plan a practical trial. Yet, as early as 1795, William Wilberforce (1759-1833), in his Diary, had described "poor Bentham " as "dying of sickness of hope deferred"; and in 1811 the scheme finally miscarried, long after Parliamentary sanction had actually been obtained for the purchase of a site. The reformer's path was throughout beset with difficulties, and, in the end, the King refused the sign manual necessary to complete the purchase and transfer of the land. "Never was anyone worse used than Bentham," wrote Wilberforce: "I have seen the tears run down the cheeks of that strong-minded man through vexation at the pressing importunity of creditors and the insolence of official underlings, Forwarding a copy to Brissot, Bentham describes the Panopticon Penitentiary as "a mill for grinding rogues honest, and idle men industrious": (Bow., x. 226.) When Burke, whom Bentham regarded as shallow and insincere, was shown the plan, he turned towards its author, saying, "Yes, there's the keeper—the spider in his Web!" The well-known scholar (1747-1819), Rector of Graffham. Parr, by his will, bequeathed a mourning ring to Bentham as "the ablest and most instructive writer that ever lived upon the most difficult and interesting subjects of jurisprudence." when, day after day, he was begging at the Treasury for what was, indeed, a mere matter of right. How indignant did I often feel when I saw him thus treated by men infinitely his inferiors."

It is true that two years later—in 1813—Bentham was awarded £23,000 as a solatium in respect of the heavy losses he had sustained; but many years after the unfortunate issue of the plan, and within a few months of his own death, its author confessed that his heart sank within him whenever the current of his thought chanced to alight upon the Panopticon and its fate. "I cannot look among Panopticon papers," he would say; "it is like opening a drawer where devils are locked up — it is breaking into a haunted house."

Bentham had not been many weeks in Russia before Wilson wrote urging him to return, complaining that he was for ever running from a good scheme to a better, and lamenting that one Paley, "a parson and archdeacon of Carlisle," had been allowed to invade his province of a reformer. The *Principles of Moral and Political Philosophy*-had, indeed, passed rapidly through two editions with prodigious applause. "It is founded entirely on utility," wrote Wilson, "or, as he chooses to call it, the will of God, as declared by expediency, to which he adds, as a supplement, the revealed will of God.... He has got many of your notions about punishment, which I always thought the most important of your discoveries; and I could almost suspect, Wilberforce's *Life,* ii. p. 71.
Published in 1785.
if it were possible, that he had read your introduction." The suggestion was that Paley must, in some way, have procured access to a stray copy of the proof-sheets— possibly one which had been sent, at Lord Shelburne's request, to Lord Ashburton, who died in 1783.2

To this letter Bentham jestingly replied that people were surprised to see how green his eyes had been for some time after its receipt—" but their natural jetty lustre is now pretty well returned. " It would seem, however, that some real impression had been made upon him by Wilson's admonition, for he, soon afterwards, writes that he is distracted to know what to do about leaving Russia: "Here I can work double tides, but, every now and then, I am nonplussed for want of books."

During the autumn of 1787 he resolved to quit CrichofT; and, in November, left Russia for England, travelling by way of Poland, Germany, and Holland. On passing through the Hague, the British Ambassador, Sir James Harris (afterwards Earl of Malmesbury), put into his hands a printed copy of the *Essay on Usury*— the first which he had seen. He reached London early in February, 1788, and secured quiet lodgings in a farmhouse near Hendon, "decently furnished with tapestry hangings, large carpets, and immense tables," where he hoped, at last, to make headway with the Code. Letter, 24th September, 1786; Bow., x. p. 163.
Letter from Wilson, 30th November, 1788. Sir Leslie Stephen points out (as Paley himself admitted) that Paley's chief source was Abraham Tucker. *Utilitarians,* i. p. 191.) Between 1786 and 1789 Bentham also wrote MSS. on the Principles of International Law. (See Bow., ii. pp. 535-71.)
Lord Lansdowne, whom Bentham, on his return home, found "vastly civil," was anxious to discover the retreat at Hendon in order to tell the recluse how much they all wished to see him again at Bowood. "He has accused himself repeatedly and *sans management"* wrote Bentham to his brother, "for not offering me a place when he was in; and commissioned me to consider what would suit me in case of his coming in again." Every week he dined at Lansdowne House; and on Jeremiah Bentham presenting to Lord Lansdowne a portrait of Jeremy, painted when a stripling at Oxford, his lordship wrote in acknowledgment of the gift: "His disinterestedness and originality of character refresh me as much as the country air does a London physician. Besides Lord Wycombe loves him as much as I do, so that his portrait will be sure to be respected for two generations."

At this period of his life Bentham, according to Bowring's narrative, made for himself a formidable enemy in the person of George III. That monarch designed to break up the alliance existing between Russia and Denmark. A private communication addressed to the Danish Court by the British Minister at Copenhagen was made public, whereupon Bentham, under the signature " Anti-Machiavel," wrote two letters to the *Public Advertiser* "shewing the causes of the unjust and useless war into which the Ministry are endeavouring to plunge us." To these letters a reply 25th November, 1789; Bowring, x. p. 225.
On the picture were inscribed a part of the copy of verses written by Bentham on the death of George II. *Vide ante,* p. 16.
appeared signed "Partizan," and Bentham rejoined in forcible and caustic fashion. A day or two after the publication of the rejoinder, Lord Lansdowne told Bentham that "Partizan" was none other than the King himself; and it was to this controversy that "Anti-Machiavel" ascribed the bitter feeling which prompted George III. to defeat the long-cherished Panopticon plan. "Who Anti-Machiavel was soon became known to this ' best of kings,' for that was the title which the prolific virtues of his wife had conferred upon him. Imagine how he hated me," said Bentham, "millions wasted were among the results of his vengeance.... After keeping me in hot water more years than the siege of Troy lasted, he broke the faith of Parliament to me." Sir Leslie Stephen treats Bowring's account of this incident with undisguised scepticism. "Lord Lansdowne," he writes, "amused himself by informing Bentham that he (Partizan) was no less a personage than George III. " However this may be, the victim of the joke never doubted the genuineness of the information given to him, and, when over eighty years of age, related the story in a volume which describes the failure of the Panopticon scheme in great detail; it is characteristically entitled, *History of the War between Jeremy Bentham and George. III. By one of the Belligerents?*
Shortly after his return from Russia, Bentham met, at Lord Lansdowne's table, Samuel Romilly, a young barrister of some five years' standing, with whom he was already slightly acquainted. "Love for pussies," so *Utilitarians,* i. p. 193. -Bow., xi. p. 96.
l.e chevalier Rtmilly fut consider!, presque dh Ventree dc sa carr tire c«mme Coracle de la hi. (kloge by Ben. Constant; MSS., Lincoln's Inn.) Ben-

tham declared, was their bond of union; anyhow, the slight acquaintance soon ripened into a close intimacy, this "love for pussies" being, as we may well suppose, a mere outward sign of that abounding love for their fellowmen which, in truth, united these eager spirits.
Another guest at Bowood was Etienne Dumont (1759-1829), pastor of the Protestant Church of St. Petersburg, and a friend of Romilly's, whom Lord Lansdowne had hoped to engage as tutor for his younger son, Lord Henry Petty. Romilly sent to Dumont, for perusal, certain of Bentham's French manuscripts; Dumont communicated extracts to the *Conrrier de Provence,* and offered to superintend the publication of the manuscripts as a whole. It is said, too, that he supplied Mirabeau with materials for some of his most renowned orations, and that these materials were, in great part, provided from the writings of the English jurist.

During many years the closest relations continued to subsist between Bentham and Dumont, the latter being constantly engaged with the ever-increasing pile of manuscripts. "The plan was," wrote Bentham to "I always enjoyed the society of tame animals," said Bentham: "Wilson had the same taste—so had Romilly, who kept a noble puss before he came into great business. I never failed to pay it my respects. I remember accusing Romilly of violating the commandment in the matter of cats.... I love everything that has four legs: so did George Wilson. We were fond of mice and fond of cats; but it was difficult to reconcile the two affections." (Bow., xi. p. 81.) Fitzmaurice's *Shelbume,* iii. p. 442. Bow., x. p. 185.
the Due de Liancourt, "that Dumont should take my half-finished manuscripts as he found them, half English, half English-French, and make what he could of them in Genevan French, without giving me any further trouble about the matter. Instead of that the lazy rogue comes to me with everything that he writes, and teazes me to fill up every gap he has observed." Bowring asserts that, in old age, the two men were "much alienated"; that Bentham was offended by some disparaging remarks as to the "shabbiness of his dinners," and, on one occasion, refused to receive Dumont. It is, probable, however, that this is a highly coloured account of some passing breach of friendship.
In editing Bentham's writings, Dumont simplified the text, softened and corrected the style, and toned down passages relating to religious topics. At times he merged several manuscripts into one, though M. Halevy, who has made a careful study of the subject, asserts that Dumont greatly exaggerated the importance of *"ce travail de fusion."* In illustration of the part played by Bentham's Swiss expositor in the production of the French editions, M. HaleVy has been at pains to collate, in parallel passages, extracts from the original manuscripts and the text of Dumont. Thus, *e.g.,* he gives a section dealing with the account to be taken of the "consequential" evil of an offence. nth October, 1795 j Bow., x. p. 313.
Bentham, *e.g.,* wrote *"dilits reJUchis"* Dumont *"dilits reflectijs ";* Bentham wrote *"satisfaction supprimatoire," "entierti dun corps du droit,"* Dumont *"satis/action suppressive," "intigraliti dun, etc"* (Hal. i. p. 376.) Mai., i. pp. 384, 385. M. Halevy also publishes a number of interesting passages hitherto unprinted. *Btntham.*—D'un délit dont résulte un mal conséquentiel, le mal total sera plus grand que s'il n'en résultoit point de tel mal. Si, en conséquence d'un emprisonnement qu'il a subi ou d'une blessure qu'il a reçue, un homme a manqué, par exemple, une place qu'on lui destinoit, un mariage qu'il recherchoit, ou un gain que lui préparait son commerce, il n'est pas besoin de dire que ces pertes ajoutées à l'emprisonnement ou à la blessure font une masse de mal plus considérable que n'en ferait l'emprisonnement ou la blessure même. *Dumont.* — Le mal total d'un délit est plus grand s'il en résulte un mal conséquentiel portant sur le même individu. Si par les suites d'un emprisonnement ou d'une blessure, vous avez manqué une place, un mariage, une affaire lucrative, il est clair que ces pertes sont une addition à la masse du mal primitif. *Traitis de Ligislation,* ii. p. 254.)
The relation between Bentham and Dumont has supplied Macaulay with a striking, if somewhat loose, analogy in his essay on Horace Walpole:—" The literature of France has been to ours what Aaron was to Moses, the expositor of great truths which would else have perished for want of a voice to utter them with distinctness. The relation which existed between Mr. Bentham and Dumont is an exact illustration of the intellectual relations in which the two countries stand to each other. The great discoveries in physics, in metaphysics, in political science are ours. But scarcely any foreign nation except France has received them from us by direct communication. Isolated by our situation, isolated by our manners, we found truth, but we did not impart it. France has been the interpreter between England and mankind."

Under continuous pressure from Bentham's friends, the pages printed so long before as 1780 were at last published in 1789, the volume being entitled *An Introduction to the Principles 0/ Morals and Legislation*

"The edition was very small," wrote the author to Lord Wycombe, "and half of it had been devoured by rats." Wilson confidently predicted that its publication would greatly raise Bentham's reputation, but his expectations were only partially realised. The book, indeed, was not, in any true sense of the word, a success. One reason of its failure to arrest public attention has been tersely indicated by Dumont in the "Discours Prdliminaire" prefixed to the *Trait/s de Legislation.* "In using several chapters of that work *(i.e.,* the Introduction) for the purpose of forming the General Principles of Legislation, I have sought to avoid that which interfered with its success—forms too scientific, subdivisions too multifarious, analyses too abstract."

Another cause to which the failure may be in part ascribed was, undoubtedly, the rapid march of events in France; the near approach of the great storm about to burst over that country and spread confusion throughout the continent of Europe.

Bow., i. pp. I—154; *vide ante,* p. 40.

Bow., x. p. 197. Vol. i. p. ix.

CHAPTER V ERA OF THE FRENCH REVOLUTION THE spring of the year 1789 found the kingdoms of Europe in commotion; the eyes of all men were turned towards France, the centre of disturbance. The States General had been summoned for the 1st of May, and Bentham, diverted for the nonce from his Panopticon proposals and the schemes of codification which had absorbed his attention, was busying himself with projects of constitutional reform. "For these five or six months past," he wrote to Lord Wycombe on the 1 st of March, "my head and my heart have been altogether in France; our own affairs, I think no more of them than of those of the Georgium Sidus."

At this time, the health of Lady Lansdowne being much impaired, her family were wintering at Saltram in Devonshire. Lord Lansdowne had indeed resolved to take his wife by sea to Lisbon, and had urged Bentham to form one of her ladyship's escort on the voyage; but this intention was never executed, as the patient's condition seemed vastly improved under the influence of the genial Devonshire climate. The rally, unhappily, was of brief duration; symptoms of great gravity *Ante,* p. 47; Lord Wycombe, said Bentham, is "as good a creature as ever breathed." presented themselves, and in a few months her disorder proved fatal. During the long illness of Lady Lansdowne, Bentham was one of the very few persons outside the family circle whose presence she would suffer; and after her death the bereaved husband constantly sought his companionship. Even amidst the anxiety and sorrow of this sad time, the interest of Lord Lansdowne was keenly aroused in the crisis across the Channel. "I am very glad to hear," wrote he to Bentham, "that you intend taking up the cause of the people in France; nothing can contribute so much to general humanity and civilisation as for the individuals of one country to be interested for the prosperity of another. I have long thought that *the people* have but one cause throughout the world—it is *sovereigns* who have different interests. "

Romilly, too, himself of French descent, had, with the assistance of Wilson and Trail, prepared for the use of the States General an account of procedure in the House of Commons, the manuscript of which was shown to Bentham. With the aid of Dumont, the tract was translated and published in France, but it is related that, when Mirabeau laid it before the Assembly at the opening of the States General, the deputies exclaimed with one accord: "*Nous ne sommes pas des Anglais, et nous n'avons pas besoin des Anglais"* They Bow., x. p. 195.

M. Halevy treats *Bentham* and Trail as Romilly's collaborators (ii. p. 32); but this seems to arise from the misunderstanding of an ambiguous phrase used by Bowring (x. p. 212). As to Trail, *vide post,* p. 132. Dumont's *Souvenirs sur Mirabeau* (Paris, 1832), pp. 160, 166; cited Hal., ii. p. 24. would not adopt my rules, said Romilly, and they hardly observed any others.

Bentham, for his part, had undertaken with his wonted zeal a treatise on *Political Tactics* which set forth the principles that govern the conduct and discipline of political assemblies, "dissecting the practice of our two Houses for the instruction of their newly created brethren." "I am labouring might and main," he explained to Lord Wycombe, " to get out some of the most essential parts at least, time enough for their meeting"; and, although the treatise was never actually published until 1816, several sections were printed and forwarded for the perusal of the Abb6 Morellet, to whom the author had been recommended by Lord Lansdowne. The Abbe observed that unreflecting persons could not possibly estimate the importance of the subject treated in this essay. "It is an instrument," said he, " by which the great victory will be won, by reason and by freedom, over ignorance and the tyranny of bad laws and vicious constitutions." Romilly remarked that he had read the *Tactics* with infinite pleasure: "all that is said about voting and debating at the same time, and about a right of pre-audience, is admirable. *On ne pent pas mieux."* Indeed, the distinguished advocate seems to have himself supplied Bow., ii. pp. 299-373.

Letter, 1st March, 1789; Bow., x. p. 197. *Essai sur la Tactique des Assemblies legislatives* (Geneva). Lord Lansdowne frequently asserted that '' the turning point" of his career was his connection with the Abbe', who "liberalised his ideas." *Memoires de Morellet,* i. xiv., cited Fitzmaurice's *Shelbume,* ii. 234.) Bow., x. p. 199. *Ibid.,* pp. 201, 264.

H certain supplemental matter for the essay, though, with his usual caution, he straightly enjoined Bentham to take care that his name should not appear.

Shortly after the meeting of the National Assembly, Dumont wrote that the plan of Parliamentary Tactics had been shown to M. de Mirabeau and the Due de la Rochefoucauld, who had both expressed admiration of the " truly philosophical conception ": in completing it, added Dumont, you will fill up one of the blanks of political literature, and no one can do it but you; for you alone have surveyed the whole field and laid the foundation of the edifice.

"To France, at that moment of delusive hope, Bentham" (says an Edinburgh reviewer) "made a generous tender of his services." Morellet strongly urged him to write on the " Theory of Representation" —a subject, said the Abbe, much discussed yet little understood—but Bentham turned towards methods of procedure and the rules of debate rather than the "composition" of the legislative body.

M. Halevy does, indeed, give extracts from MSS. in University College written in French, which show that Bentham *was,* at this time, contemplating a distinctly radical essay on " Representation." It is suggested by M. Halevy that, although he was not as yet a believer in democratic government, Bentham was writing for Mirabeau, and so approached the subject from his point of view. "For France, the constitution that the Father Letter, 27th Sept., 1789; Bow., x. p. 219. Chapter vi. of this essay—"Mode of Proceeding"—was printed in quarto, 1791. Vol. xxix. p. 218. The reviewer was, we believe, Romilly.

of the People should strive to establish is simply a pure democracy, but under the shelter and protection of a monarchy"—he wrote—"... The English Constitution is admirable for the English or for the French. The American Constitution is, in itself, still better, but it would not suit either of those nations."

But, in Bentham's view, political liberty depends upon the free action of the "public will," which, in turn, depends in large measure upon the *mode of procedure* observed by the Assembly. The importance of uninviting forms is, therefore, no fine-spun speculation—no fanciful conceit. "In this bye-corner, an observing eye may trace the original seed-plot of English liberty: it is in this hitherto neglected spot that the seeds of that invaluable production have germinated and grown up to their present maturity, scarce noticed by the husbandman, and unsuspected by the destroyer. "

The National Assembly had not been long formed when a new organisation of the *judicial* establishment was proposed by the Constitutional Committee. Bentham at once set to work to examine the proposal and suggest modifications. His criticisms and comments are contained in a work entitled, "*Draught of a Code for the Organisation of the judicial Establishment in France,* with critical observations on the draught proposed by the National Assembly Committee," which was printed in numbers but not at that time published. An extract from the manuscript appeared, with grateful acknowledgment, in Mirabeau's journal, the *Courrier de Provence,* No. 121, etc. (Seances du Lundi 22 au 23 mars 1790, Hal., i. p. 434. Bow., ii. p. 332.

p. 123), and on the 1st of April a hundred copies were sent to the President of the Assembly. On the same day Lord Lansdowne wrote to the Due de La Rochefoucauld commending to him Bentham's proposals as deserving more than ordinary attention. The author, he explained, had for several years devoted his whole time to the study of general principles, and was " by a hundred degrees, the most capable person in the country to judge of the subject."

This letter discovers, incidentally, the high esteem in which Bentham was at that period held by the writer. A year before, Colonel Bentham had been assured by his brother that Lord Lansdowne was as zealous as himself for universal liberty of government, commerce, and religion, and for universal peace; while the terms of this letter make manifest the close bonds of personal affection—not merely the looser ties of intellectual sympathy. "I love him," avowed Lord Lansdowne, "very tenderly as a man, to the full as much as I admire him as an author, and look up to him as a lawyer."

On the 26th of August, 1792, at the instigation of his friend and admirer, Brissot, the National Assembly bestowed on Bentham the title of Citizen of France, and on the 9th of September charged the executive authority to inform him of their decree. The Assembly, on the same occasion, was pleased to confer a like Bow., iv. pp. 285-406. A French edition appeared in 1823.

Bow., x. p. 226. Charles Abbot (Lord Colchester) asserted that he had heard Lord St. Helens speak of Bentham as "the Newton of Legislation." *(Ibid,,* p. 238.) *Ibid.,* p. 217. *War,* wrote Bentham, *is mischief on the largest scale.* distinction on Washington, Priestley, Wilberforce, and a few other foreigners, who had served the cause of liberty and rendered themselves worthy of the title by their sentiments, their writings, or their valour. Notifying his acceptance in a letter to the Minister of the Interior, Bentham observed with discretion and dignity that, if he were to consider himself thereby released from any of the duties contracted towards the country in which he was born, he would give but feeble evidence of fidelity in the discharge of new engagements. "If unfortunately I were forced to choose between incompatible obligations imposed by the two positions, my sad choice, I must own, must fall on the earlier and stronger claim.... Passions and prejudices divide men; great principles unite them. Faithful to these— as true as they are simple—I would think myself a weak reasoner and a bad citizen were I not, though a royalist in London, a republican in Paris. I should deem it a fair consequence of my being a royalist in London that I should become a republican in Paris. Thus doing, I should alike respect the rights and follow the example of my sovereign who, while an Anglican in England, is a Presbyterian in Scotland, and a Lutheran in Hanover." In this same letter Bentham makes a forcible plea for the exercise of clemency towards the *emigr/s,* urging that they should be allowed to return to France; the marked differences which separated their political opinions from his own weakened, in no way, the sentiments of sympathy inspired by their woful plight; to some of them, indeed, he was at that Bow., x. p. 281. time extending generous hospitality. Punishment that is not necessary, he insisted, is in all cases *lawless* punishment; in civil war the end is answered when the minority is subdued; the victims are too few to be proscribed as a measure of precaution, too many to be sacrificed as a measure of punishment.

It has been remarked that the *Draught of a Code for the Organisation of a Judicial Establishment* was one of the first signs of the conversion of Bentham towards more democratic views; and, in truth, we may readily trace in certain passages of this treatise the germs of many of those luminous ideas which, thirty years later, were to be developed by him so admirably in his criticisms of our own judicial system. To us English, he explains, a system of local judicature, distributing justice upon the spot in all its branches, is new, not only in practice, but even in imagination. With us no man has yet been found bold enough to insinuate that fifty pounds in costs may be too high a price to pay for five shillings, or four hundred miles too far to go for it!

Commenting on the project of the National Assembly, he seems to have thought it necessary to adopt— though, as he afterwards asserted, much "against the grain "—the principle of popular election as applied to judges, the choice to be made without any control by the executive government. He was willing, even, to invest the people with a power of removal, accounting "probity" as of more importance than "independence" in the judicial equipment. "It is surely a bold experi Hal., ii. p. 25.

Letter to Dumont, October 19th, 1802; Bow., *x.* p. 399. ment," he wrote, "this of trusting the people at large with the choice of their judges: the boldest, perhaps, that was ever proposed on the popular side. My thoughts were divided betwixt the King and the representative assemblies. I could scarce think of looking so far down the pyramid as to the body of the people. But now that the Committee has given me the courage to look the idea in the face, I have little fear of the success."

"Happy France!" he cried, in commenting on the decision of the Committee that all subjects without distinction should plead in the same form and before the same court: "Happy France! where aristocratical tyranny is laid low; while in England it is striking fresh root every day. When a peer commits a murder, more mischief is done by his trial than by his crime.... To the nation, the life of an idle peer is worth as much as that of an idle porter, but not so much as that of an industrious one." He admitted that the right of being tried by their own body in capital cases had been of use to peers so long as they remained in a state of perpetual hostility with the Crown, to which juries were subservient. But in modern times this privilege had become naught but a burden to the nation—by reason of the time and money wasted in the formalities of investigation—and of use to nobody, unless it be to the Lord Chamberlain, and to make a raree-show! Bow., iv. p. 309. Francis Horner, referring to this tract, speaks of "its irresistible effect in setting the mind of the reader to work by the boldness and restlessness of the writer's speculations. It is the most effectual exercise in the art of legislative reasonings." (Mem. and Corr., i. p. 427, cited Hal., ii. p. 374.) Bow., iv. p. 321.

Yet Bentham, now well past forty, was still far removed from the Radicalism of his later years; his eloquent advocacy of innovation had hitherto been inspired by eagerness for legal reform rather than by zeal for the cause of liberty. Indeed, at no period of life were red ruin and the breaking up of laws at all to the mind of Jeremy Bentham. Macaulay claims him as one of the " illustrious reformers" who were brought to a "conservative" frame of mind by the "excesses of the French Revolution"; but, at the date of the Revolution, he was, in no real sense, a *political* reformer. It is true that MSS. written by him in French and recently brought to light by M. Halevy show him, even then, ready to criticise *"le galimatias de la representation virtuelle,"* and to look favourably on secret voting and the suggestion of a *reduced* franchise.2 So long as a man has *any* assured property to lose, however small, argued Bentham, there is no fear of his fancying it in his interest to ally himself with those who possess nothing at all, for the purpose of bringing about an equal division of property: since this, indeed, means nothing less than the destruction of all property. But he had passed his sixtieth year when first he showed any disposition to give active support to Parliamentary reform; and it is certain that, long before the Jacobins demanded the death of Louis, he had declared that the constitutional branch of the law of England, taking it in its leading principles, would probably be found the best beyond comparison that had hitherto Essay on Sir James Macintosh's *History of tlu Revolution,* edition 1865, p. 316. Hal., i. p. 435 made its appearance in the world, resting at no very great distance, perhaps, from the summit of perfection. Favoured are the people whose happiness it is to have stumbled upon such a possession!

The truth is that, throughout the whole era of the Revolution, while taking no part in the fierce polemics of the time, he adopted an attitude aptly described as one of "hostile indifference" to the tenets of the Jacobins.'We can imagine that he might, if asked, have defined his position in some such words as these: "' Fraternity,' if you will; but 'Equality,' no! it would need violence to preserve it — and as to 'Liberty,' subjection, not independence, is the natural state of man."

Enunciating his theory of the *ownership of property,* Bentham—inspired by Hume—recognises the principle of "security" as fundamental; he is, it is true, very far from ignoring the principle of "equality," but, when "security" and "equality" are in opposition, there should, he says, be no hesitation—" equality" must give way. Security is the foundation of life, of subsistence, of abundance, of happiness; the establishment of equality is a chimera, the only thing which can be done is to diminish inequality. It is, as Professor Montague most justly observes, this profound sense of the need of security which to some extent made up for Bentham's *"Of the Influence of Time and Place in Matters of Legislation."* (Bow., i. p. 185, where the passage first appeared in English. The manuscript was, in later life, marked by Bentham in red ink, "written in 1782,' and the passage appeared in the *Traitls* (1802) in a greatly modified form: *La brancke constitutionelle des lois d' Anglctcrre est admirable a plusiers igards,* etc., vol. iii. p. 371.) Hal., ii. p. 20. » Ct MSS. cited Hal., i. p. 422.

Bow., i. p. 311. lack of historical insight, and preserved him from the adoption of extreme revolutionary doctrines. Liberty he asserted to be neither more nor less than the absence of coercion—the idea of it is purely negative—it must be considered as a branch of security. *Personal* liberty is *security* against a certain species of injury which affects the person, while *political* liberty is *security* against the injustice of the members of the Government. Political liberty he regarded as merely a relative good, one of the means of attaining to happiness, the sole object of real value. *Liberty* subsists by the restraints not being imposed upon ourselves. *Security* is produced by restraints being imposed on others. Where there is no coercion there is none of that liberty which is produced by law. "Is it by all coercion, then, that liberty is produced? By no means. It is only by restraint. Is it, then, by all restraint? Is it by restraining a man from any sort of acts that it may be produced? By no means. But of those acts alone by which, were he to do them, he would restrain the liberty of another man; and then it is plain, it is not in that man whose acts it restrains that it produces liberty, but in the other. "

In the year 1793 Bentham addressed to the National Convention of France a pamphlet on the fallacy of Colonial monopolies entitled *Emancipate your Colonies!* "shewing the uselessness and mischievousness of dis Montague's *Fragment on Government,* p. 38.

Bow., i. p. 302. *Traitis de Legislation, Discours Priliminaire,* i. p. xvi. MSS., Univ. Coll. (No. 69), cited Hal., i. p. 360. tant dependencies to a European State." Trade, so his argument ran, is the child of capital. Yes, it is the *quantity of capital,* not *extent of market* that determines the quantity of trade. Here are you engaged in producing, for the consumption of your colonies, goods in the manufacture of which you are excelled by other countries: England, for example. You ought to be producing goods in which you succeed better than England. People in England, on the other hand, being, to this extent, kept from producing the goods they can succeed best in, are turned aside to the production of those in which they do not succeed so well: and thus it is all the world over. Will you believe experience? Turn to the United States. Before the separation, Britain had the monopoly of their trade; upon the separation, of course, she lost it. How much less is their trade with Britain now than then? So far from being less, it is much greater.

All this while, is not your monopoly against the colonists clogged with a *counter monopoly?* To make amends to the colonists for their exclusion from other markets, are not you forbidden to take certain produce from other countries, though you could get it ever so much cheaper? Yes, the *benefit* is *imaginary,* and it is clogged with a *burthen* which is Printed in 1793, py given to Talleyrand's secretary, but not published for sale until 1830: Bow., iv. pp. 407-18. Bentham's views on this subject were shared by Lord Lansdowne, who, during a debate in the House of Lords in 1797, said that no greater evil could happen to England than that of adding the Spanish colonies in South America to our already excessive possessions. (Hal., ii. p. 36, citing *Ann. Reg.,* 1797, p. 186.) *real.* The thesis of this little work Bentham shortly afterwards described as one of his Jacobinisms, though, as we have already seen, he was, at that time, no radical; he was, in fact, strongly averse from the theory of the " rights of man."

So early as 1789 he had written to Brissot: "I am sorry you have undertaken to publish a Declaration of Rights. It is a metaphysical work, the *ne plus ultra* of metaphysics. It may have been a necessary evil— but it is nevertheless an evil." On the 20th May, 1793, he sent to Dundas a copy of his pamphlet on the Colonies, together with a copy of the *Parliamentary Tactics* and of the treatise on *Judicial Establishment.* Referring to these books and to another tract which accompanied them, Bentham observed: " Some of them might lead you to take me for a Republican—if I were I would not dissemble it: the fact is that I am writing against even Parliamentary Reform, and that without any change of sentiment." Indeed, two years after Bow., iv. p. 413. The author prophesied in 1829 that, before the end of the nineteenth century, Australia would have emancipated herself and become a representative democracy. He made, also, an interesting observation as to Egypt: "It would, without doubt, have been *advantageous to Egypt* to have remained under the government of Great Britain—a government which would have bestowed upon it peace, security, the fine arts, and the enjoyment of the magnificent gifts which nature has lavished upon it. But, in respect to *wealth,* the possession of Egypt, far from being advantageous to England, would have proved only a burthen." *(Manual of Political Economy,* Bow., iii. p. 53.) Henry Dundas *(1142-1811),* first Viscount Melville, afterwards impeached for gross malversation, but acquitted by a majority of his peers. He lived to vote against Romilly's Bill to abolish the death punishment for stealing 5;. in a shop.

Bow., x. p. 293. Bentham was seeking for employment in the preparation of statutes, or on legislation for Hindostan. the date of this letter to Dundas, we find that he was contemplating a reactionary essay, to which he proposed to apply the characteristic title *"Rottenness no Corruption,* or a *Defence of Rotten Boroughs,* by the author of the *Defence of Usury."* The course of events in France was, also, supremely distasteful to him; in the confiscation of church property and the restitution of estates to the descendants of Protestants persecuted under Louis XIV., he perceived an attack upon the principle of "security"; the impassioned eloquence of the orators of "la Constituante" served only to irritate him. He would have joined an association directed against the spread of Republican propaganda but for a chance meeting with Romilly in the street; he undertook the preparation of a treatise designed to expose *Anarchical Fallacies,* and described as "an examination of the declaration of rights issued during the French Revolution." The recognition of the nothingness of the laws of nature, and the rights of man that have been founded on them, is, said he, of much importance. "Natural rights is simple nonsense: natural and imprescriptible rights, rhetorical nonsense — nonsense upon stilts. But this rhetorical nonsense ends in the old strain of mischievous nonsense: for immediately a list of these pretended natural rights is given, and those are so expressed as to present to view legal rights." This tract is contained in the second volume of the collected works, but the MSS. lay unpublished, and, indeed, unprinted, for many years. What Bowring MSS., Univ. Coll. , No. 43, cited Hal., ii. p. 311. Hal., ii.

p. 35. Bow., ii. pp. 489-534; edited from the original MSS. describes as "a feeble version" was included by Dumont, in a volume published by him at Geneva. Curiously enough Dumont's version appeared, together with *Political Tactics,* in 1816, at a time when, as Sir Leslie Stephen points out, Bentham was himself accepting the practical conclusions of this much-criticised declaration. According to Macaulay, it was intended to establish "that the atrocities of the Revolution were the natural consequences of the absurd principles on which it was commenced; that, while the chiefs of the constituent assembly gloried in the thought that they were pulling down aristocracy, they never saw that their doctrines tended to produce an evil a hundred times more formidable, anarchy; that the theory laid down in the Declaration of the Rights of Man had, in a great measure, produced the crimes of the Reign of Terror. " The tract really contains little more than verbal criticism: Look to the letter of the declaration, and you find nonsense—says the author—look beyond the letter, you find nothing!
Although, as we have seen, Bentham at this period took no part in active politics, he suggested, in the year 1796, that some attempt should be made to establish friendly relations with France. He made to Wilberforce a futile proposal that they two (being probably the only English "French citizens" who were not "reputed Republicans") should set out on a mission to Paris. "What say you, then," he wrote, " to an expedition to Paris upon occasion, properly dubbed and armed, not *Utilitarians,* i. p. 218.
Essay on Mackintosh's *History of the Revolution,* edition 1865, p. 316. *d la* J n, to *devour* the country, but *d la* Wilberforce, to give *peace* to it? The knight of Yorkshire, at any rate—his *fellow-citizen,* if so it please his knightship, in quality of his humble squire to keep his *armour* in order and brush his shoes?. .. True it is that were they to see an analysis I have by me of their *favourite Declaration of Rights,* there is not, perhaps, a being upon earth that would be less welcome to them than I could ever hope to be *(sic)*; but there it lies, with so many *other* papers that would be equally obnoxious to them, very quietly upon my shelf; and though no man can be more averse to *simulation,* even in the best cause, yet no man, according to my conception, is bound to *suppress* any ideas that he happens to have *in common* with those whom his business is to conciliate, still less to *fling at their heads* any that he happens to entertain in *opposition* to theirs, because no man is bound to get his head broke to no use. " Needless to say, nothing came of this strange project, which was pronounced by the experienced diplomatist, Lord St. Helens, to be wholly unseasonable; although he allowed that the proposal exhibited Bentham in no other colours than his true and proper ones, of a most zealous and disinterested *Publicolist.* In the then humour of the French, it seemed to Lord St. Helens impossible to prevent such a compliment wearing the appearance " of a most unworthy and degrading compliance with their arrogant and unwarrantable pretensions."
The momentous political movements, which stirred *Quare* Jourdan. Bow., x. pp. 316, 317.
(7SJJ9-) See his interesting letter to Bentham, Bow., x. p. 319. so profoundly the continent of Europe and excited so lively an interest in Bentham, were accompanied by considerable changes in his own personal and family affairs. Until the death of his father in 1792, he continued to lodge on the farmstead near Hendon, seeing nobody, reading nothing, and writing books which nobody read. The lodging was very pleasant, in a pretty country—" all in grass "—and the farmer's wife was a good cook. He had, too, given some sixty guineas for a "superb" harpsichord, with four strings to every note—" an elegant piece of furniture, very beautifully inlaid," which had been made in 1781, and cost originally nearly double that price. The tone, he declared, was very sweet; but he doubted whether he should not have preferred a " simple grand pianoforte," which was to be had for the same money and possessed a louder tone. The farm is the first house, or rather hut, you come to, when you have passed the eight-mile stone on the way to Mill Hill, he explained to his brother: "At Hampstead you have only to ask the road to Hendon; it is the great one." Even more precise are the directions supplied to the Colonel when, in May, 1791, he had reached Paris on his return from Russia: "Have a letter ready for me in your pocket to inform me of your arrival; if it is at the general penny post-office, in the Haymarket, before 9, or at least before 7, I shall have it the next day between 12 and I, if I happen to walk to the office—if not, between 1 and 2.... Name your hour and I will meet you at Highgate Church, which is a pleasanter road than Romilly's *Memoirs,* vol. i. p. 417.
Hampstead. If I am not there at the time, come on to the White Lion; inquire your way to Finchley Church, and when you are there for *Dallies.* In the great northern road, about a mile or a mile and a half beyond Highgate, in the way to Barnet you will come to a nursery ground. At the top of the hill, on the lefthand, is a public-house called the Bald-faced Stag; at the bottom before you come to the Bald-faced Stag is another—the sign, the White Lion I believe. Close to this White Lion is the stile that goes to Finchley Church, which is about a mile distant."

Having conceived a strong desire to enter Parliament, Bentham, in August, 1790, addressed a letter of no less than sixty-one pages to Lord Lansdowne, reproaching that nobleman for neglecting to execute a supposed promise to provide the necessary pocket-borough. Somewhat tiresome by its prolixity, this letter is yet well worth reading, as exhibiting at once many of the excellences of the writer's earlier style, as well as his curiously defective perception of the ways of the world and of the motives which guide an ordinary man of affairs.

"That it was a decided offer, which, when coupled with acceptance, makes a promise, I could not suffer myself to doubt. One thing only prevented me from regarding it as an *unconditional* and *immediate* one. The only vacancy apparently in view was that which

seemed the natural result of your breach with Colonel Barre I could not tell, from anything you had at that In the earlier letter he warned his brother to take the Hampstead road, "as the other would be unfindable." (Bow., x. p. 248.) Elected for Chipping Wycombe in 1761, in succession to Lord Shelburne, who never actually took his seat in the Commons. (Fitzmaurice's *Shelbume,* i. p. 118.) M. P. for Calne 1774-90. *Vide ante,* p. 65.
time said to me, whether this breach was absolutely irreparable: I could not tell whether, in the event of its being irreparable, some positive engagement or notions of expediency might not induce you to leave him in possession of his seat." A livery, my dear lord —remarked Bentham in a later passage of the letter— should have wages, at least where they have been promised; and he goes on to relate how the Duke of Somerset, "upon meeting with I don't know what disappointment from George II.," carted his liveries with great parade to the palace and shot them down in the courtyard. "My livery will not be shot down in the courtyard: it shall be laid down silently in the drawer, with a God-bless-him to the master who once chose that I should wear it."

Referring to his own qualifications for parliamentary life, the writer urges that, though speaking and writing are very different things, it does not follow, because a man has been thought to write tolerably well, that he should be pronounced incapable of speaking. "Or is it that a man who studies his parliamentary or other business is a pedant, and a pedant is not fit to sit among fine gentlemen; and altogether the fitter a man is for the business of Parliament, the less fit it is for you to put him there? This I suspect to be the logic that has overpowered the united force of affection, principles, and justice."

To this effusion Lord Lansdowne replied next day with conspicuous restraint and much good feeling, disclaiming any promise or engagement, and adding a solemn assurance, on his word and honour, that he had never made any such offer as was supposed. The same reasons which induced his correspondent to decline the practice of his profession had applied—so Lord Lansdowne understood—in large measure to a parliamentary career: a view in which he was strongly confirmed by repeated conversations in which Bentham had stated his happiness to depend on his perfect independence, and declared that his every aspiration was centred in his particular pursuits.

"The moment you mentioned Parliament to me in town, you were witness to my astonishment, and it fully explains the forgetfulness you mention, which you attribute to affectation, certainly not one of my failings.... Now that I know your wishes, I assure you that it will give me great pleasure if I can contribute to the completion of them; and that I will spare no pains for the purpose, so far as consists with the engagements I have expressed or implied, which have taken place when I was totally ignorant of your inclinations.... I am now only afraid that you will be angry that your sixty-one pages have not, on the one hand, had the effect of subduing or terrifying me; or, on the other, made me angry; and that you apprehend them to be thrown away. They have not occasioned to me one moment's irritation, but they are not thrown away. I select with satisfaction the seeds of esteem and regard which I perceive interspersed....

"As to ebullitions, I am myself subject to them; and, though they are more momentary, they are not half so ingenious, and, therefore, not half so pardonable. You may, then, depend, whatever you say or do, upon my remembering nothing, but how truly I am your affectionate, humble servant—Lansdowne."

To this kindly reply the rejoinder could hardly fail to be conciliatory:—

"My Dear, Dear Lord,—Since you will neither be subdued nor terrified, will you be embraced? These same seeds you were speaking of have taken such root, the ground is overrun with them; and there would be no getting them out were a man to tug and tug his heart out. So Parliament may go to the devil, and I will take your Birmingham halfpence, and make a low bow, and put them gravely in my pocket, though they are worse than I threw away before."

But, though his wrath was turned away, Bentham added somewhat disingenuously, as it would seem—

"Offer? Why no, to be sure it was not. Why, didn't I tell you I only called it so for shortness? More shame for you that you never made me any.... It was using me very ill, that it was, to get upon stilts as you did, and resolve not to be angry with me, after all the pains I had taken to make you so."

The writer concludes with an inquiry as to when the doors of Bowood would be open to him—provided always that no " fair hands" had barred them against him—and Lord Lansdowne at once replies: "I leave it to you to make the application. If you make it rightly, you will make it unnecessary for me to keep the ladies waiting dinner longer, in order to assure you how affectionately and unalterably I must be always yours."

On his return to England in the summer of 1791, Colonel Bentham was included in the invitations to Lansdowne House and Bowood, and was informed by his brother that he would there find ladies prepared to like him, "but proud, and virgins, and the most terrible of prudes." "When these three Dianas get together," complained Bentham to one of them, "the ice becomes even colder; they are like snow, saltpetre, and sal-ammoniac" j yet, on the 25th June, he writes to Lord Lansdowne: "I wonder what ladies there are at Bowood, and whether there be any part of the summer when a man would stand a chance of seeing them all three. I worship but at one altar: but that, as everybody knows, has three sides to it."—" I shall be in Wiltshire," replied his hospitable friend," before the end of July, so, if you have any devotion in you, you may acquit yourself of it either in August, September, or October, as you feel disposed towards the three Deities, who have chosen a month apiece in their natural order; and if your brother is not too much captivated with

Lady M to endure the simplicity of your religion, he will be very welcome. "

At the same time the brothers were receiving pressing invitations to pay a long visit to Antony House, near Plymouth—its owner, Sir Reginald Pole Carew, sharing their interest in chemical and physical research and in the progress of mechanical invention. The Bow., x. p. 267. Presumably Miss Caroline Vernon, Miss Elizabeth Vernon, and Miss Caroline Fox.
Carew, who had met Samuel Bentham at St. Petersburg, was a warm partisan of the Panopticon scheme, and served on the committee which undertook in 1797 (with Charles Abbot as chairman) to report on the plan. first note, dated 14th June, 1791, begins: "Oh! that I had legs like my friend Bentham, said I, when strolling about this evening, then would I never be at rest," and relates that the writer had just established a new ferry from Plymouth Dock to Torpoint, about a mile and a half from his house. The invitation was renewed on the 22nd July. "As I am come a great way, so would I stay a great while to receive you here.... I take the opportunity of sending you this *lettre de cachet,* enjoining you and your brother to render yourselves here instantaneously, upon pain of incurring our high displeasure; *et sur ce je prie Dieu de vous avoir dans sa digne et sainte garde. A vous."*
Colonel Bentham, who alone was able to avail himself of their friend's hospitality, received, while in Cornwall, a letter from Jeremy, making arrangements for the projected journey to Bowood, which contains, by the way, a curious reference to the ill-starred Panopticon scheme: "Cast about with Carew all sorts of measures that appear to hold out a chance of bringing Panopticon to bear here;—the bribery plans, for example, in the event of its not getting a hearing otherwise. This as from yourself: anything of that sort will come better from an intriguing Russian like you, than from a reformer like your betters."

The promised visit to Lord Lansdowne was paid in the late autumn of this same year (1791), and Bentham seems to have greatly enjoyed the diversion, if we may judge from the jocular tone of the letters written afterwards from Hendon to the ladies of Bowood and Warwick Castle. To Lady E. G. (probably Lady Elizabeth Greville, then a child of some twelve years) he writes: "Honoured Madam!—May it please your Ladyship! I am the young man who was taken from behind the screen by my good Lady Warwick, in the room where the pianoforte is in Warwick Castle, to wait upon your sweet person, and had the honour and happiness of accompanying you with the violin in one of Signor Bach's sonatas." He trusts her ladyship's condescending goodness will excuse his freedom in addressing her, as he thereby makes bold to do, for, being out of place and turned adrift upon the wide world, he wishes for the felicity of serving her ladyship in the capacity of musical instructor, or in any other of which he should be found capable. "I served the Hon. Miss Fox, whom belike your ladyship knows—she being, as I am informed, your ladyship's cousin-german,—for ten long years, and hoped to have served her till death, had I not been, with grief be it spoken, forced to quit her service by hard usage. She was a dear lady, and a kind compassionate good lady—as I have heard everybody say, and to be sure so it must be, as everybody says so—to everybody but poor me. To be sure it must have been my own unworthiness, therefore it would be very unreasonable of me to complain." Two days later he makes bold to inform "Honoured Madam" that "my lady" and he had made it up, and she had given him his due and more, too, wherefore he had altered his mind, meaning no offence; and so on.

A few weeks after the date of these letters, the ladies of the Lansdowne family seem to have denied themselves to Bentham, and he thereupon addressed to them a lengthy plea or protest which, although written in a lively strain, clearly manifests considerable resentment. "Believe me, you can scarcely be more awake to what may be, or may be thought, propriety on your part, than I am. But, unless some recent aversion be at bottom, I really cannot find out what it is your delicacy, three of you as you are, could have had to apprehend from a man like me.... Do you fear my becoming troublesome? correct me, or even discard me at any time. Whatever place I may have enjoyed in your favour, I am, and ever shall be, your debtor for; your grateful and insolvent debtor. The smallest hint from Lord Lansdowne would do it—this would be the gentlest of a thousand modes.... Some of you, I doubt, were not chidden quite so severely, some years ago, as you ought to have been, for tearing flies' wings off, or holding them in the candle."

The response to this protest was an immediate invitation, but the intimacy thus renewed was not of long duration.

During the year 1791, Jeremiah Bentham, seeking the restoration of his health which had become much impaired, had gone to reside at Bath, where he died in the month of March, 1792. His property was equitably divided between his two sons, Jeremy's inheritance comprising—in addition to the estate of Queen's Square Place in Westminster—freehold and leasehold property yielding from £500 to *£600* a year, a considerable portion of which, consisting of farms in Essex, had been purchased by his grandfather. Being now in possession of ample means, he quitted the farm at Hendon for Queen's Square Place, where, in his garden, was preserved a small house reputed to have been occupied by John Milton during the time in which he acted as secretary for Cromwell. Bowring describes it as "an obscure brick house," partially concealed by a fine sycamore tree in a corner of the garden; and relates that on the occasion of his first visit to Bentham, his host suddenly stopped in front of the sycamore, laid his walking-stick—" Dapple "—on his guest's shoulders, and cried, " On your marrow-bones, sir!" at the same time pointing to a slab which bore the inscription, "Sacred to Milton, Prince of Poets."

Lord Lansdowne had heard the news of the old man's death and wrote counselling Bentham to visit Paris, "the greatest scene which can come within the human comprehension." After enlarging upon the beauties of a "cottage" which he had just purchased, on the coast lying between Christchurch and Lymington, the writer added," This cottage is, therefore, quite at your service; but what is there here to keep pace with all we hear?—a *pavilion! wines innumerable;* a *table so plentiful, and yet so refined; such selection of company.. ..* Tell your brother whenever he wants to rest his appetites from such profusion, I hope that he knows where he will be extremely welcome."

Bentham made answer: "O the tyranny of the aristocracy! Give it a furlong, and it will take a mile—a veto stopped me once from going to Brussels, and now There were barracks adjoining, whence issued—to Bentham's horror —the cries of soldiers being flogged in the yard.
comes a *Lettre de Cachet* ordering me to Paris.... At present, the pavilion is turned into an hospital for refugees. Vaughan consigns me a cargo on Saturday. I have obligations of the same sort to Dumont; and now, while I am writing, comes a note from Romilly, announcing similar ones for to-morrow; and what after all if I should have to house poor L. Rochefoucauld instead of his housing me?"
Nothing apparently could exceed the cordiality of this correspondence; yet the same summer witnessed the determination of those intimate relations between Bentham and the Lansdowne family which had subsisted for ten long years. The estrangement—for it was in no sense a rupture—was deeply deplored by Bentham, and its cause does not seem to have been placed on record. "Invitations ceasing," he wrote thirtysix years afterwards, " so of necessity did my visits to Lansdowne house. Other incidents such as, if related, could not in any the smallest degree be discreditable to any one party concerned, but which neither time nor space would allow me in any other way so much as to glance at, cannot but have contributed to this everlamented effect."

Some say that invitations ceased by reason of the divergent views of the two men on current political topics; by others it is suggested that a coolness arose Benjamin Vaughan *('751-1835),* a loyal supporter of Lord Shelburne; M.P. for Calne 1792; emigrated to America 1798.
Rochefoucauld was killed in September of the same year. *"Vous deviez fire h diner chez Bentham,"* wrote Dumont to Romilly on Ilth September, *"qunnd on a appris ct M. de Liancourt la mort horrible de M. di la Rochefoucauld."* (Romilly's *Memoirs,* it p. 6.) from Lansdowne's neglect of the Panopticon scheme. May it not be that Bentham, emboldened by accession to comparative wealth, had made advances to Caroline Fox such as proved unacceptable to that lady and rendered habits of close intimacy in some sort embarrassing? When—a few months after Lord Lansdowne's death in 1805—there came, as we have seen, a formal proposal of marriage, Miss Fox told Bentham that they could never meet *but as friends,* adding significantly: "*This* I did think that, *after a separation of sixteen* (? thirteen) *years,* we might have done with comfort and satisfaction to us both. " Little light is thrown upon the subject by the extant correspondence: the few letters addressed to Miss Fox during their early intimacy are written, for the most part, in a strain of banter, though, as their writer himself remarks, the mere turn of a sentence has decided the fate of many a friendship, and, for aught we know, of many a kingdom. The point of the allusion is often lost to us for want of the necessary clue, yet some of the persiflage still remains amusing enough, thus: "Do you know why it was Jephthah sacrificed his daughter? Was it that he wanted to get rid of her? No such thing.... Why then? Because he had said he would; and, if he had not been as good as his word, he would have been accused of inconsistency, he thought, and of want of perseverance, in all the Jerusalem newspapers." Prudence, said he in another passage, would have condemned the whole of this letter to the flames; but, if ever the time should come, when one J. B. is able to write, or speak, or behave to a Miss F. or a Miss V., as he does to others, or as others do to them, it will be a sign that the reign of attractions and fascinations is at an end, and that F. and V. are become no more than A., B., or C. A few passages may, however, be found which suggest that there lay beneath this raillery an undercurrent of deeper feeling; in one letter, for example, he begs the favour of a note from her in these words: "Tell me, said I, nine days ago, either that I have not offended, or that I am forgiven. Ten days which have elapsed since have lowered my pretensions. Tell me now, it would be a kindness done to me, that I *have* offended and am *not* to be forgiven.... My great employment has been hunting for grounds of self-accusation—no very pleasant one while the bushes are beating, and still less when game has been found. If I have offended, has not the punishment been sufficient?"
Whether our surmise as to the cause of this unfortunate estrangement be correct or not, there was manifestly no personal feud, for two years later we find Lord Lansdowne writing: "I have, I assure you, been in a great deal of pain for you, for I am afraid you have got among a set of r s. I have been perpetually thinking how I could be of use to you. The ladies are out of town. Why will not you and your brother come and dine here some Saturday with Romilly and Dumont, vhen it can do you no harm to talk your affairs over?" Lord Wycombe, too, who was staying in Italy during the Letter December I2th, 1794; Bow., x. p. 306. Lord Lansdowne refers to the difficulties which had arisen from the Panopticon scheme.
autumn of 1795, kept up a friendly correspondence with Bentham, sending him long gossiping letters descriptive of the various incidents of his travel. And many years afterwards, in the summer of 1812, an invitation came from the then Marquis of Lansdowne —the "little Henry" of former days—summoning his old friend to take possession of the apartment at Bowood, which, for a generation, had gone by his name; but Bentham could not find time to obey the summons, nor did he ever again enjoy the shelter of that hospitable roof. Bow. , x. p. 472. CHAPTER VI FIFTEEN YEARS'

WORK ON LEGAL
REFORM (1793-1808)

"HE history of the unfortunate Panopticon scheme, which disturbed Bentham's peace of mind for more than twenty years, has been already sketched in brief outline; and it would be at once tedious and unprofitable to trace in detail the course of his gallant struggles against an adverse fate—the end, as we have seen, was failure and financial disaster.

In 1813, it is true, he secured a large sum by way of compensation for his losses. "Oh, how grating— how odious to me is this wretched business of *compensation!"* he exclaimed: "Forced after twenty years of oppression—forced to join myself to the *Baal-peor* of bloodsuckers." And it was, indeed, a cruel stroke of fortune which compelled him to contribute—as he put it—to the impoverishment of a public he had fondly hoped to benefit by a signal service; but no less than fifteen years earlier he had been driven to seek refuge in his brother's house. "While others are proving their loyalty by their affluence," he wrote, in despair, to George Rose of the Treasury, " I who have nothing left but loyalty, am reduced to shut up my house (the residence of the family for three and thirty years), fortunate in finding a brother's to take refuge in."

However, neither his long absorption in this prison project, nor his constant excursions into French politics, prevented him from making large additions to the swelling piles of manuscript. A few of his productions were printed with a view to immediate publication; a number were handed over to Dumont or some other disciple, while many still lie in the British Museum or at University College. He engaged in the preparation of tracts on a great variety of subjects; indeed, the habit of neglecting the Code for passing events of less enduring interest had become inveterate—he was for ever turning down one bypath or another.

In December, 1792, he wrote a trenchant pamphlet, in the form of a running commentary upon a charge to the Grand Jury of Middlesex, delivered on the 19th November by Sir William Ashhurst, a puisne judge of the King's Bench. Ashhurst's charge had been printed at the instance of the *Constitutional Association* of that time and industriously circulated, but Romilly advised that publication of the pamphlet was not likely to do good and might do harm: "The praise given to the French would, I have no doubt, throw discredit on all the truths it contains." Bentham's references to France and its code, being few in number and capable of ready excision, must have been seized upon by Romilly as a pretext for the suppression of certain forcibly expressed home-truths as to English February 23rd, 1798; Bow., xi. p. 116.
law and English lawyers, which would, in those days, have rendered publication highly perilous to the author.

"Why is it that, in a court called a court of *equity,* they keep a man his whole life in hot water, while they are stripping him of his fortune?" inquired the writer: "Take one cause out of a thousand. *Ten* appointments have I known made for so many distinct days before a sort of judge they call a *master,* before one of them has been kept. *Three* is the common course; and as soon as everybody is there, the hour is at an end, and away they go again. Why? Because for every appointment the master has his fee. Some of these law places are too good to be left to the gift even of judges: of these, which bring in thousands upon thousands a-year, the plunder goes to dukes and earls and viscounts, whose only trouble is to receive it. In France, no fees to judges, no selling of law places. Is it not this, for one thing, makes lawyers so eager to support Ministers in their schemes for cutting the throats of the French?— the French, who whatever mischief they have done to one another, have done none to us, but love and respect us." The pamphlet was not actually published until 1823, when it appeared under the title of *"Truth v. Ashhurst; or, Law as it is Contrasted with What it is Said to be.* "

In the following two years Bentham turned his attention to f1scal questions. An essay, printed in 1793 and published in 1795, was entitled, *"A Protest against Law Taxes,* showing the peculiar mischievousness of all such impositions as add to the expense of appeal to Bow., v. pp. 231-7.
justice." "It is" (wrote the *Edinburgh Review* on the appearance of a second edition in 1816) "a work, which, for closeness of reasoning, has not perhaps been equalled, and for excellence of style has never been surpassed; a chain of political argument, as close and as beautiful as anything which the severest of the sciences presents."
Taxes on consumption, the author declared, fall on bodies of men who are quite able to protect themselves, while the oppressed and ruined objects of the taxes on justice are condemned to weep alone in holes and corners. Suitors for justice have no common cause, and scarce a common name. What does a Chancellor of the Exchequer care for them? They are everybody and nobody. A tax on tobacco falls upon a man immediately and presses on him constantly; everyone knows whether he means to sell or use tobacco. "A tax on justice falls upon a man only occasionally: it is like a thunder-stroke which a man never looks for till he is destroyed by it. He knows not when it will fall on him, or whether it ever will: nor even whether, when it does fall, it will press upon *him* most or upon his adversary. He knows not what it will amount to; he has no *data* from which to calculate it; it comes lumped to him in the general mass of law charges: a heap of items, among which no vulgar eye can ever hope to discriminate: an object on which investigation would be thrown away, as comprehension is impossible. Calamities that are not to be averted by thought are Bow., ii. pp. 573-83. Dumont inserted an abstract in an Appendix to *Traiti dts Preuves Judiciaires* (1823). Merely putting in an answer to a bill is said to have cost, in one case, more than;£8oo. (Bow., ii. p. 583.) K little thought of, and it is best not to think of them. When is the time for complaint? Before the thunderbolt is fallen, it would be too soon—when fallen, it is too late."

It was reckoned that the expense of carrying through a common action to recover the most trifling sum could not be less than *£24* on the plaintiff's side alone; and at the time when Bentham wrote, a further extension of the taxes on law proceedings was impending. Upon those even who had the wherewithal to pay, such an imposition was grievous enough; to those who had not, these impolitic taxes were neither more nor less than a denial of justice. *Justice shall be denied to no man, justice shall be sold to no man,* runs Magna Charta. Denied it is, said Bentham, to nine-tenths of the people; to the remaining tenth it is sold at an unconscionable price—a sale by the State as pernicious, in point of political effect, as one for the benefit of a king or a judge.

George Rose displayed great interest in the subjectmatter of the pamphlet and affirmed, in the presence of Pitt, that there should be no more law taxes; but we still await the complete fulfilment of his promise.

Bentham wrote and sent to Charles Long a paper which was shortly afterwards published under the title Bow., ii. p. 581.

Bow., xi. p. 122. George Rose (1744-1818) was for many years Secretary to the Treasury. *1J61-1838.* Joint Secretary to the Treasury, afterwards Lord Farnborough. "The work that was to be done was concocted by Rose—the secret superintendence of the workmen was managed by Long." (Bow., x. p. 308.) of " *Supply without Burden; or, Escheat* vice *Taxation* being a proposal for the saving of taxes by an extension of the law of Escheat, including strictures on the taxes on collateral succession comprised in the Budget of 7 Dec, I79S" The tract purports to resolve a riddle which its author had propounded to Long in these terms: "What is that pecuniary resource of which the tenth part would be a tax, and that a heavy one, while the whole is no tax, and would not be felt by anybody?" The answer afforded was, in substance: "An extension of the Law of Escheat whereby property would revert to the State in case an *intestate* died leaving only *distant* relations." Bentham proposed to draw the line at degrees beyond which marriage is no longer forbidden; such relations as did not stand within the prohibited degrees he termed *without the pale* and proposed to exclude. He maintained that, when once this alteration of the law had come into actual operation, there would be little or no feeling of *disappointment* among those excluded from succession; that, even as the law stood, the distance of relationship, in many cases, precluded expectation on the part of remote kinsmen. Hardship, he contended, depends upon *disappointment; disappointment* upon *expectation; expectation* upon the dispensations—that is to say, the *known* dispensations—of the law. He had no wish to impair, in any degree, the liberty of a testator in regard to the free disposal of his estates by will where such disposition was in favour of children or near relations. Bow., ii. pp. 585-598, cf. Rom. *Mem.* ii. p. 106. As an "aid to the operation" of his main proposal, he did, however, suggest a certain *limitation* of the power of making bequests in favour of persons *without the pale.* (Bow., ii. p. 586.)

He recognised, moreover, that the operation of succession laws, regulating the devolution of an intestate's property upon members of his family, was in full accord with the principle of" utility," the children being thus maintained in that state of life to which their father's wealth had called them. The daughter of a labourer, left penniless, will go forth to her labour without any sense of disappointment and, perchance, without a murmur of discontent; not so the rich man's daughter, reared in ease and opulence. But there is a vast difference between *children* who have shared their father's fortune and the *distant relations* unearthed by some enterprising attorney to assert a claim of kinship. The exclusion of such relations from a share in their kinsman's riches, while adding to the resources of the State, would inflict no conceivable injury or hardship upon any individual. Supply without burden, exclaimed Bentham, is victory without blood. But the plan presented grave difficulties; and it would have been no easy matter—if, indeed, at all possible—(as his friend James Trail shrewdly observed) to convince *the public* that the suggested mode of raising supplies would be less burthensome or oppressive than a slight tax on collateral succession.

The administration and reform of the Poor Laws was one of the many subjects which, at this period, engaged Bentham's attention. Towards the end of the eighteenth century the strict principles of the Eliza Barrister; M.P. for Oxford; died 1809. "He was," said Romilly, "a very remarkable instance of a man most eminently qualified to have attained the highest honours of the profession... but no attorney ever discovered his merits." (Rom. *Memoirs,* i. p. 434.) bethan Poor Law had, by slow degrees, been greatly relaxed. "The labour test prescribed by the Elizabethan law was falling into disuse, and it had become customary to give outdoor relief in money payments to the ablebodied and infirm alike without distinction." Gilbert's Act (1782), intended as a temporary expedient during the distress caused by the American War, enabled assistance to be given, in such parishes as adopted its provisions, without applying the workhouse test. No doubt, as sometimes happens at this day, hardship had resulted from the refusal of occasional relief to the industrious poor—relief such as was best suited to meet the needs of the particular case; but the main—if not the sole—object of the innovations seemed to be the alleviation of existing destitution, and nothing more. Indeed, it has been well observed that the Poor Laws and their administration had come to be regarded by the Government simply as a means to prevent discontent from developing into despair and revolution. It is true that the treatment of the "deserving" poor was receiving some consideration from the public; but the difficulties of that perplexing problem, still unsolved, were almost ignored by the Legislature.

Bentham was one of the first to perceive that the mere giving of relief to the suffering afforded a wholly unsatisfactory basis for the solution of the many difficulties that had arisen. There must, he clearly saw, be restrictions framed to check the growth of pauperism by *English Local Government* (Redlich and Hirst), i. p. 1o1.

Cf. Stephen's *Utilitarians,* i. p. 93. *English Local Government* (Redlich and Hirst), i. p. 88. a rigorous application of the labour test, by the segregation of such as might be shown to be incorrigible vagrants, and by a sustained effort to improve those susceptible of improvement: the education of the poor he conceived to be of far greater moment than the education of the rich.

In the early part of 1797 a Poor Law Bill, which Pitt had introduced in the Commons the year before—on a plan suggested by Mr. Ruggles, a country gentleman of Essex—was criticised in considerable detail by Bentham, who submitted his manuscripts to the promoter of the Bill. Pitt's measure fell through, and its abandonment seems to have been largely due to Bentham's luminous *Observations;* but it comprised several projects still worthy of passing notice in view of modern political developments. There was, for example, a scheme for supplementing wages by affording relief to every man who could not earn "the full rate or wages usually given in his Parish,"—the "Under-Ability, or Supplemental Wages Clause," as Bentham called it; another for providing money to paupers to enable the purchase of a *cow,* for the constant maintenance of which, says Bentham, "about *three acres* of land is looked upon as necessary." Both these projects were denounced in forcible terms— the one as "equalisation," the other as "sentimentalism"; both as unfair and impracticable. The Bill also proposed to create something analogous to Old Age Pensions, by the provision of what Bentham described as "annuities humanely destined to diffuse a gleam of comfort over the evening of life." The manu Bow., viii. pp. 440-61.

Plans, said he, *for throwing the parish upon the parish.* script appears to have lain unpublished until 1838, when Edwin Chadwick issued the *Observations* in the form of a pamphlet for private circulation.

But Bentham did not content himself with a mere criticism of other men's proposals. He propounded an elaborate plan for a uniform national system under a non-official board; suggested the location and detention of beggars and other vagrants in workhouses, unless they could find security ensuring that they would engage in labour elsewhere; and (amongst other innovations) advocated—as in the case of the Panopticon— the *contract,* as distinguished from the *stipendiary,* system of management, on the *duty-and-interest-conjunction* principle. The directors of a joint-stock company were, indeed, to act as the central authority.

The scheme was first made public in the autumn of 1797, and appeared in Arthur Young's *Annals of Agriculture. A* "Succedaneum to Pitt's Poor Bill" it was styled by its author, who (amongst other things) urged the establishment of "Frugality Banks" on lines coincident, in the main, with those upon which the Legislature proceeded on the creation of Savings Banks. His plan—wrote Chadwick forty years later—contained the anticipation of those improvements which a long period of trial suggested in the institution of banks of this character; indeed, the *whole system* with its deferred annuities and other characteristics may, as Hill Burton has said, be found distinctly set forth in the papers contributed by Bentham to the Annals. He *1800-1890.* Chief Commissioner for Poor Law, 1833; knighted, 1889! Cf. Bow., viii. pp. 361-431; *Tracts on Poor Laws and Pauper Management.* also urged that, as a further encouragement to frugality, facilities should be afforded for the transfer of small sums of money from place to place such as are now enjoyed under the modern system of post office orders. Romilly gives us a glimpse of Bentham "locking himself up at Hendon" to complete his Civil Code; but, during the last two or three years of the eighteenth century, we find him engaged on a curious variety of topics. His friend Patrick Colquhoun, a police magistrate, who had been a Glasgow trader, was commissioned to report on the best means of increasing the efficiency of the Police; and, with Bentham's assistance, a Bill was prepared, which took the form of the Thames Police Act, 1800. At the same time a scheme was elaborated for the prevention of forgeries, and suggestions were made for the manufacture of a sort of icehouse, or "Frigidarium," for the purpose of preserving fruit, vegetables, and other fermentable substances. In November, 1800, a long letter, written by Bentham under the signature of " Censor," appeared in Cobbett's *Peter Porcupine.* It related to the method of taking the census, and was addressed to Charles Abbot, who had introduced his "Population Bill" into the House of Commons. Many of the hints contained in this letter were acted upon, and the suggested improvements adopted in obtaining the census returns. Proposals were also made for the conversion of Stock into An Bow., viii. p. 417.

1745-1820. Author of the *Treatise on the Police oj the Metropolis;* "he hit the mark by pushing in *quart,* where learning would have missed it by pushing in *tierce,"* said Bentham. It is said that between February, 1800, and April, 1801, more than one hundred persons were executed in England for forgery. nuity Notes—a project which Bentham contended was quite free from risk, would benefit small holders and prove superior to the Exchequer Bill system. The treatise embodying these proposals is styled—*"A Plan for saving all trouble and expense in the transfer oj stock, and for enabling the proprietors to receive their dividends without powers of attorney, or attendance at the Bank of England, by the conversion of Stock into Note Annuities"* The author—who was of opinion that Government ought to have the monopoly of Paper Money as well as of Metallic Currency—proposed that the State, after the manner of private banks, should issue notes for small sums; the notes issued by the State to carry interest daily from the date of issue. This essay was printed in part, and the whole scheme submitted to George Rose on the 3rd January, 1801.

In the year 1802 Dumont at last gave to the world the result of his labours on the Benthamic manuscripts. The *Trait/s de Legislation* passed through the press in the spring, and was published at Paris in June, three months after the Treaty of Amiens. "It is very entertaining to hear Bentham speak of it," wrote Romilly to Dumont: "He says that he is very impatient to see the book, because he has a great curiosity to know what his own opinions are upon the subjects you treat of." Dumont himself was confident of success, and declared that the author of the *Vue GMrale dun Corps Complet de Legislation* would certainly be placed at an infinite distance above all who had preceded him.
Bow., iii. pp. 105-53; cf. letters to Sir F. Baring, x. p. 340.
Mim., ii. p. 75.
The work appeared in three volumes, which contained—" *Principes du Code Civil"* and "*Principes du Code Penal,"2* the latter code being subdivided into four parts—" *Des D/lits," "R/mides politiques contre le tnal des D/lits," "Des Peines," "Des Moyens indirects de prevenir les D/lits."* There were published in this treatise, in addition to the two Codes, "*Principes de L/gislation," " Vue G/nirale d'un Corps Complet de Legislation!" "Promulgation des Lois, etc.," "De 1'Influence des Terns et des Lieux en matiere de Ligislation," " Code Penal—Titre Particulier,"* and a Memoir upon the Panopticon scheme.

It will thus be seen that Bentham's survey covers a field of vast expanse; and, in truth, many a salutary modification of our system of jurisprudence may be traced to the ideas enshrined and developed in these volumes. His conclusions, explained Dumont, apply alike to a monarchy or a republic: he does not say to the people, "Change your rulers," but to the rulers, "Study the remedy for the ills that afflict your people." He rent asunder, wrote Bulwer Lytton, the fantastic and illogical maxims on which technical systems were founded, he derided their absurdities and exposed the flagrant evils which in practice they pro
Vol. ii. pp. 1-236; Bow.,i. pp. 297-358.
Vol. ii. pp. 239-434, and vol. iii. pp. 1-200. Adaptations from the *Introduction* (1789). Bow., i. pp. 367-86. *It.*, pp. 533-78.
Vol. i. pp. 1-140.
/A., pp. 146-370; Bow., iii., 154-210.
Vol. iii. pp. 275-301; Bow., i. pp. 158-63.
'Vol. iii. pp. 325-95; Bow., i. pp. 172-94.
Vol. iii. pp. 302-321; Bow., i. pp. 164-168.
Vol. iii. pp. 209-75.
duced. Perhaps his grandest achievement, Lytton continued, was "the example which he set of treating law as no peculiar mystery, but a simple piece of practical business, wherein means were to be adapted to ends, as in any of the other arts of life."
No part of the work is more luminous, or possesses greater living interest, than the author's enunciation of the general principles of punishment. These principles were borrowed in some measure from Helvtius and Beccaria, and nowadays are commonly accepted; yet it needed no little courage to advance them when the theft of a chicken from an enclosed yard was a capital offence, and there was everywhere a strong disposition towards the view of Sir Leicester Dedlock's relative: " Far better hang wrong fellow than no fellow at all."

Romilly, in his charming diary, relates a striking instance of the prevalent savagery: One evening in June, 1808, after the introduction of his Bill to abolish the death penalty for pocket-picking, while he was standing at the bar of the House, a young man, the brother of a peer, came up to him and, breathing in his face the nauseous fumes of an undigested debauch, stammered out, "I am against your Bill; I am for hanging all. " Romilly was confounded, sought to find some excuse for him, and observed that he supposed the young man meant that, as the certainty of punishment afforded the only prospect of suppressing crimes, the laws, whatever they were, ought to be executed. "' No, no!' was the reply; 'it is not that. There is no Article in *England and thi English,* 1833, by Bulwet Lytton, assisted by J. S. Mill; reproduced in Mill's *Early Essays,* by Gibbs(l8o7), at p. 390. good done by mercy; they only get worse. I would hang them all up at once.'" Even Bentham himself regarded the conviction of an innocent man with an indifference which is somewhat surprising. "He calmly weighs in his balance," wrote an Edinburgh reviewer, "the *inconvenience* of condemning the innocent against that of suffering an offender to escape."

Montesquieu, a magistrate by profession, had adhered to the ancient doctrine of retaliation—an eye for an eye and a tooth for a tooth. He regarded it as obvious and indisputable that the penalty for stealing goods should be the forfeiture of other goods. He opined that "when one intelligent human being has inflicted injury on another, the former deserves *me'rite)* to suffer a like injury. " But Bentham saw clearly enough that the use of this word " *me'rite "*—this talk of an offence as " deserving" punishment, as "being equivalent" to the penalty—could lead only to error and confusion. Following Beccaria, he denounced, as a false principle that had long reigned a tyrant throughout the vast province of penal law, this "reasoning by antipathy," as he phrased it: for it is but an irrational subjection to the blind impulses of anger and revenge which have in all ages obscured the vision of judges and legislators.4 Penal Vol. xl. p. 179.
ibSg-1755. Prisident h mortier in the Parliament of Bordeaux. *1735-1794-* His treatise on Crimes and Punishments was published in 1764. *Traitis* (Principes de Legislation), i. p. 122. The *Tkeorie des Peines,* in which the matter is further discussed, was declared by Romilly to possess ' very extraordinary merit," and to be likely to make '' a very deep impression." When it appeared in 1811 a reviewer, referring to Bentham's treatment of this subject, wrote: "It has been impossible for us to give even a specimen of the rich vein ot illustration which runs through the legislation before Bentham's days, said Sir Samuel Romilly, resembled what the science of physic must have been before physicians knew the properties and effects of the medicines they administered.

It is the *effects* we must assess and ever keep steadily in view; the effects alike of the wrong done and of the penalty proposed. The beneflt of mankind by the repression of crime is the *ultimate* object of our penal codes, and this must not be lost sight of while pursuing the *immediate* object, which is the punishment of the individual culprit. The real end to be attained is the protection of society, not the torment of an offender.

From the point of view of "utility," indeed, all punishment is in itself an *evil,* for every punishment involves the infliction of pain, and pain is an evil. It would therefore be unwise to attempt the enforcement of *every* moral precept by means of some prescribed penalty, since the enactment of a fixed and positive punishment for a noxious action of slight and varying importance, or of a private nature, might well create a greater evil than the one sought to be suppressed. "Penal law," said Bentham," can only be applied within certain limits." Its power, for example, extends only to palpable acts or omissions susceptible of manifest proof: or there may, perchance, be an insuperable difficulty in subjecting the offence to such clear and precise definition as would guard effectually against misapplication whole of the original treatise. Examples are never wanting from the laws and the history of all ages and nations to explain and to enforce the general positions. The work in this department has a manifest superiority over Montesquieu's celebrated performance." *(Edin. Rev.,* vol. xxii. p. S7.) of the law, as in the case of rudeness or ingratitude. Again, the fear of detection may be so slight as to raise but little expectation of punishment in future instances of similar delinquency, as in the case of illicit commerce between the sexes, unattended by any act of violence or public indecency. *La legislation, en un mot, a bien le mime centre que la morale, mais elle n'a pas la mime circonftrence.*

On the other hand, a crime wrought for but small individual profit may entail widespread suffering; and the punishment, albeit attended by pain to the delinquent, must be brought into correspondence with the aggregate resulting effects, regard being had only to the general advantage. Moreover, an offence already committed may concern a single individual alone, yet the commission of similar offences may affect all men. *L'affaire pass/e n'est qu'un point, mais I'avenir est infinir*

Punishment, then, while it must not be in excess of that which is absolutely necessary, should, so far as may be, suffice for the prevention of similar offences. In many cases, after the commission of an offence, it will be found impossible to redress evil already wrought, but it is always possible to get rid of the inclination to repeat the offence; for, howsoever great may be the "profit" resulting from crime, the " pain " of punishment may always be made to preponderate. The "profit" of a crime is the force which urges a man to delinquency; the " pain " of the punishment is the force employed to restrain him from it. We must then see to it that the second of these forces is the greater, otherwise the *Trailis,* i. p. 98. *Hid.,* ii. p. 292.
crime will be committed—that is to say, committed by those who are restrained by the laws, and not by such tutelary motives as benevolence, religion, or honour.

Appropriate legal punishments, says Bentham, are services imposed on those who undergo them for the good of society; and regarding them in this light, one speaks of the punishment allotted to a criminal as a debt which he owes and must needs discharge.

But were public opinion to tolerate the exaction of a most savage and inhuman penalty, it is all important to remember that the mere risk of incurring even such a punishment would fail to operate as a complete deterrent—the Nemesis is too uncertain to restrain those helpless, hopeless wretches from whom the ranks of crime are, in the main, recruited.

It is, therefore, not merely on the restrictive action of the sanctions, in relation to this or that particular offence, that dependence must be placed. We must seek to eliminate, so far as may be, the criminal propensities of the individual, to induce and encourage habits of thought alien from crime; and, in this way, to weaken or destroy the potency of seeming temptations. While advanced age will not yield to new impressions, youth may be moulded like wax; many crimes are not deeply rooted in the heart—they spring up from seduction, example, and, above all, indigence and hunger. Some, again, are but sudden acts of vengeance which do not imply habitual perversity. When the angel Gabriel prepared the prophet Mahomet for his mission, the story goes that he took out of Bow., i, p. 500.
his heart a black spot which contained the seed of evil. Unhappily, says Bentham, this operation is not practicable in the hearts of ordinary men; but while the punishment is being undergone, *reformative* influences may be brought to bear upon the delinquent, he may be induced or compelled to engage in work— the mode of treatment being adapted to his mental or moral condition — and so out of the *evil* of the punishment there will spring positive *good,* a gain alike to the offender and to society at large.
Thus the problem resolves itself into a particular case for the application of the general principles of the "moral arithmetic," and we see how these ideas of punishment became fundamental to the Benthamic-' penal code. The theory, as we have said, was largely borrowed from Beccaria. In what, then, does the originality of Bentham consist? It consists, as M. Hal6vy points out, in a superior faculty of logical arrangement destined to make him one day master of a school of thinkers. Beccaria, who sketched the ideas in outline, did not approach Bentham either in rigorous definition of the principles or in the systematic development of their far-reaching consequences. Bentham, says Professor Montague, grasped with astonishing firmness axioms which Beccaria had merely indicated with the light touch of an essayist. Hal., i. p. 100; and cf. *Edin. Rev.,* voL it p. 28. "In England the philosophical element of the movement *(i.e.* abolition of capital punish-

ment) was nobly represented by Bentham, who, in genius, was certainly superior to Beccaria, and whose influence, though perhaps not so great, was also European." (Lecky's *Rationalism in Europe,* voL i. p. 349.) *Fragment en Government,* p. 32.

Barbarous as were the provisions of our criminal code at this period, it is, perhaps, worth while to note that they had become largely inoperative. Judges and jurors alike rebelled against a too rigorous enforcement of the law; as is ever the case, any attempt to exact a penalty grossly disproportioned to the offence served only to shock the general sense and to excite a spirit of compassion with the accused. Between 1803 and 1810 great numbers of prisoners were found not guilty and discharged; and, though no less than 1,872 persons were sentenced to death for petty thefts and divers small offences against property, one only of those sentences was, in fact, executed. Bentham was among the first to denounce this condition of affairs, and to point out that the *certainty* of a comparatively slight penalty would prove a far more efficient check than the *possibility* of a most extravagant punishment. The more certain we can make the punishment, the less may its severity be: "*Plus on peut augmenter la certitude de la peine, plus on peut en diminuer la grandeur.*"

Nor should we omit to relate how Bentham insisted that acts of *cruelty to animals* must be classed among crimes or offences cognisable by law; the word *crime,* said he, being incurably indistinct and ambiguous, is the word to be employed on all rhetorical occasions. He foretold the coming of a time when humanity shall stretch her mantle over everything which breathes; yet it was half a century before the Legislature of his own country made any real attempt to recognise its fundamental duty in this regard, and, though a further halting *Traitis,* ii. p. 387.

L step was taken in 1900, the prophecy is, to-day, far from complete fulfilment. Many an act of gross barbarity still finds no place in the category of punishable offences.

In Bentham's view, men may be allowed to kill, or inflict pain on, animals with a determinate object, if that object be beneficial to mankind and there is a reasonable prospect of its accomplishment; but no man should be suffered to torment them. Why, he asked, should the law refuse its protection or deny its aid to any sensitive being? With characteristic vigour he urged the suppression of *all* forms of wilful cruelty, *soit par maniere d'amusement, soit pour flatter la gourtnandise."* Under the guise of "sport" to beguile the leisure of the rich or idle, cock-fighting, bull-baiting, fox-hunting, coursing, all entail the most exquisite suffering and the agonies of a prolonged and painful death. Even the milder pursuits of shooting and fishing are, at times, attended by incidents such as clearly reveal the presence of some degree of brutality, or, at least, a marked absence of reflection on the part of those who engage in them. Nor should the Legislature, he contended, restrict itself solely to *prohibitive* decrees: the death of animals may be rendered less painful by the adoption of many simple processes well worthy of being studied and of becoming "*un objet de Police."*

If, moreover, humanity to animals—the sentiment of benevolence—were inculcated in the minds of children, would it not tend towards the prevention of crimes of violence, "*ou du moins de prevenir cette dipravation Traitis,* iii. p. 124.

brutale qui, aprh sitre joute des animaux, a besoin en croissant de s'assouvir de douleurs numaines"? On the 15th June, 1809, the House of Commons was engaged in rejecting a Bill which proposed to make it an offence maliciously to wound horses, cattle, sheep, or swine. During the course of the debate, Sir Samuel Romilly remarked that nothing could be more just than the observation of a distinguished painter (Hogarth), who, beyond all others of his profession, had devoted his talents to the cause of morality: the artist, in tracing cruelty through its different stages, had represented it as beginning with delight in the sufferings of animals and ending in the most savage murder. Cruelty to animals, observes Lecky, naturally indicates and promotes a habit of mind which leads to cruelty towards men.

Dumont's hopes of success were in large measure realised, and on the appearance of the *Trait/s,* Bentham rapidly acquired renown. "You will be pleased," wrote Lord Lansdowne to Lord Holland," that Dumont and Bentham's book is likely to make its way and lay the foundations of a new science in Legislation." For the purpose of introducing Charles Fox, Dr. Parr had taken him to the author's door. Writing to complain that Bentham abruptly "ran away" to avoid the introduction, Parr added: "I am sure you would not have been sorry to hear what passed between him (Fox) and myself about your mighty talents, your *Trait/s,* i. p. 107. Bentham had already referred to this subject in the *Introduction* (1789), Bow. , i. pp. 142-3. In 1798 was published the second edition of *Pity's Gift,* intended to excite "the compassion of youth for the 'Animal Creation.'" April 13th, 1803; Fitzmaurice's *Shelburne,* iii. p. 569.

profound researches, your important discoveries, your irresistible arguments. " Sir Frederick Eden declared that Dumont had collected a glorious harvest of Bentham's sowing: "If life be, in truth, divided into pain and pleasure," said he, "Bentham has certainly much increased our stock of the latter." Romilly, the overworked lawyer, who bore the marks of toil "but too conspicuously in his face," talked of translating the book into English. "To do him justice," said Bentham, "I mean in point of sanity—it must have been rather in the way of *velUit/* than *volition."*

"Anne told you, I believe," wrote Romilly to Dumont on the 31st May, 1803, "that there is no mention of you in the third number of the *Edinburgh Review.* I don't think you have any reason to be sorry, unless you think it would be of use to your book to have it abused. The editors seem to value themselves principally upon their severity." However, the criticism, which ultimately appeared in the seventh number (April, 1804), though adverse, cannot fairly be described as hostile. The reviewer maintained that the judgment of the legislator should be directed rather by the common impressions of morality, the vulgar distinctions of right and wrong " as Nephew of the first Lord Auckland; author of *History of the Labouring Classes,* etc.; organiser of the Globe Insurance Office. Died 1809.

Romilly's *Memoirs,* ii. p. 104. In January, 1798, Romilly had married one Anne Garbett, whom he had met at Bowood. Presumably Thomas Thomson: see *Memoirs of Francis Homer,* i. p. 236. Thomson *(1768-1852)* was appointed deputy clerk-register in 1806, but removed in 1839: *(National Dictionary of Biography.)* to which all men are agreed," than by the "oracles of utility." He took leave of the publication "with some feelings of fatigue," but was, nevertheless, so obliging as to lay down his pen " with sentiments of the greatest respect for the talents of the author." Dumont, who had merely heard rumours of these strictures, wrote to Bentham: "I am charmed that the lessons of these young people have come in time to prevent me from continuing my follies. I only just wait to read what they say, before I throw all your MSS. into the fire. What remains of life will be tranquil." Within ten years of the appearance of this criticism, the *Edinburgh* referred to the *Traitis* as that " admirable volume "; and, indeed, had declared, as early as 1809, that Bentham had in that treatise done more to elucidate the true grounds of legislative interference than all the jurists who had gone before him.

The book had an immediate and considerable sale in Russia. The Empress Dowager expressed a wish that Dumont, who was paying a visit to St. Petersburg in 1803, should be presented to her, and orders were given for the preparation of a careful rendering of the *Tra: 't/s* into the Russian tongue. "I desire for my country," wrote General Sabloukoff, "the possession of those truths which the beneficent genius of Bentham has created for the whole human race. Russia wants Bow., x. p. 415. VoL xx. p. I.

Vol. xv. p. 101. See the review, by James Mill, of Bexon's *Theorie de la legislation Fenale:* Jeffrey had struck out all Mill's references to Bentham, but himself inserted this declaration: (cf. Bow., x. p. 452). Brougham characterised the praise as "excessive " and " not very consistent with the former article." *(Ibid.,* p. 454.) laws. It is not only Alexander the First who desires to give her a code—Russia herself demands one.... Let Jeremy Bentham prepare it!" A large number of copies were sold in the Spanish Peninsula, where translations of several of Bentham's works appeared; indeed in 1822, the Cortes of Portugal decreed the rendering of his works into Portuguese at the expense of the nation. Blanco White, editor of the *Espaftol,* bore testimony to the effect produced by the writings in Spain: "Though thwarted in their circulation by prejudice and ignorance, they were looked for and read with avidity; they were mentioned as a leading rule for the amendment of our laws, when a committee was appointed to that purpose, during the Central Junta." In Italy, Greece, and even South America, Bentham's books rapidly became known, and in 1810 he wrote—with a vanity almost childlike—from the "Hermitage," as he styled his house in Queen's Square Place: "Now at length, when I am just ready to drop into the grave, my fame has spread itself all over the civilized world; and, by a selection only that was made A.D. 1802, from my papers by a friend, and published at Paris, I am considered as having super To General Bentham, 5th February, 1804; Bow., x. p. 413. Admiral Modvinoff wrote: "I am laying up a certain sum for the purpose of spreading the light which emanates from the writings of Bentham. " *(Hid.,* p. 419.) Cf. Borrow's *Bible in Spain,* ii. p. 276. An Alcalde, whom the author met in 1837, spoke of "the grand Baintham who has invented laws for all the world.... The most universal genius which the world ever produced—a Solon, a Plato, a Lope de Vega.... I possess all the writings of Baintham on that shelf, and I study them day and night." Bow., xi. p. 20. *Ibid.,* x. p. 456. seeled everything that was written before me on the subject of Legislation." And, in truth, the boast had very solid foundation. It was avowed, in the none too friendly pages of the *Edinburgh Review,* that his reputation had become "thoroughly European," though he had been left almost "a stranger in his father's house." While his fame and the knowledge of his great qualities have been growing abroad, "we have been amusing ourselves," wrote the reviewer," like the *valet-de-chambre* of a hero, with his foibles and peculiarities at home.... This singular state of exotic reputation (a sort of juriconsultal bishopric *in partibus transmarinis)* is not, however, a matter of accident or jealousy. Strange as in England it may sound to ordinary ears, and even ridiculous to legal ones, they have got an idea on the Continent that there is such a thing as the Philosophy of Legislation."

In 1805 Lord Lansdowne had died at the age of sixtyeight, and in the same year, as we have already seen, Bentham made an offer of marriage to Caroline Fox. These proposals were rejected in terms that left no doubt as to their finality; but the rebuff administered to him in no way impaired Bentham's energy or diverted him from his great purpose. So far from being driven to "muse and fold his languid arms," he was soon engrossed in a conspicuously prosaic subject, to wit, "Reform of the Scottish Judicature." The *Edinburgh Review* had published an article by Jeffrey, in which the great Scotch lawyer speaks of Bentham as a profound Letter to his cousin Mulford who "bad a notion that whatever was in print was a lie." (Bow., x. p. 458). VoL xlviii. p. 458.

and original thinker, cites lengthy passages from the *Draught of a Plan for the Organisation of Judicial Establishments,* and expresses a hope that he may be induced to write on the subject of the proposed reform of the Court of Session. His assistance in the matter was, in fact, sought by Lord Grenville, apparently on the suggestion of Lord Henry Petty; and a series of papers was soon prepared in vigorous denunciation of the astounding condition of affairs then prevailing in Scotland—the enormous expense, the great delay, the elaborate treatises laid before the judges in the form of pleadings compared with which the declarations and pleas of an English court seemed simplicity itself. How, asks Bentham, shall we extract a simple system of pleading?" Comyns, title *pleader,* shall be taken into the laboratory. It shall be thrown into the roasting furnace; the arsenic, 60 per cent., will fly off in fume; it shall be consigned to the cupel; the lead, 30 per cent., will exude out and repose for everlasting in the powder of dead men's bones. The golden button, 10 per cent., shall be gathered up and made the most of."

More than one bold attempt, undertaken at this period, to obtain legal reforms of the highest consequence is connected inseparably with the name of Samuel Romilly. Some of the attempts met with partial success, and Bentham justly claimed to share in the glory associated with these enterprises—in par Vol. ix. p. 462. Jeffery *1773-1830)* became a judge of the Court of Session in 1834.

Bow., v. pp. 1-60. *Ibid.,* p. 28. ticular, with the projects for tempering the severity of an inhuman penal system. Bentham's influence upon his friend was both direct and profound. *"Jamais-filiation d'id/es,"* says M. Halevy, *"ne fut plus facile a suivre."* Manuscript writings, rough fragments, printed proofs were all alike at Romilly's service. "Having given to the matter," wrote Bentham, "that softening which his temper suggested and policy required, illustrating and enriching it with such facts as his experience had brought within his observation, Romilly made it up into one of those pamphlets which bear and do so much honour to his name."

In the year 1808 Bentham made the acquaintance of James Mill, the historian of British India, who at this time resided in Stoke Newington, whence he came with some frequency to dine at Queen's Square Place, usually calling on his way to spend an hour with Francis Place at his shop near Charing Cross. The enormous influence which, towards the end of his life, Bentham exerted upon liberal thought in England was, says Mr. Graham Wallas, largely due to his constant association with a number of able men, some of whom always enjoyed the "most complete intellectual intimacy" with him and with each other: "Of these men the ablest was James Mill."

The summer months were spent at Barrow Green, about half a mile from Oxted. Bentham speaks of the Manor Farm where he lodged as " a very pleasant abode Hal., ii. p. 280.

MSS., Univ. Coll., No. 132; cited HaL, ii. p. 369. *Life of Place,* p. 65. Mill was born in 1773 and died in 1836. in warm weather," standing in a place that was once a park and still bore a "park-like appearance": it was in the possession of the tenant for life, a widow whose first husband (one Hoskins) had been the lord of Barrow Green and other manors. She was not only her own housekeeper but her own cook—and a good cook too, taking " great pride and delight" in the culinary art. One of the two halls which this ancient homestead boasted was hung around with the horns of deer chased in former days on the neighbouring hills. Outside the house, a spreading lawn stretched away to the shrubbery; and beyond, a long straight avenue of chestnut trees, which Bentham called "the cloisters," led down to the margin of a lake some seven acres in extent and well stocked with various kinds of fish. The smooth surface of the water was broken here and there by clusters of reeds and bulrushes; there was an island in the centre, and the banks were skirted by clumps of trees and tangled thickets. At some distance from the house, on the further side of the public road, was a large kitchen garden protected by walls on every side, but the fruit trees had in later years been much neglected. "About half a mile beyond the lake," wrote Bentham, "rises a range of hills, very bold, with here and there chalk pits, here and there woods with pleasant walks in them and very extensive prospects, exhibiting gentlemen's seats in abundance." To this old manor house Bentham invited James Mill and his family in the summer of 1809, when the intercourse between the two men gave rise to a close Bow., K. p. 436. friendship, and produced on the mind of the older philosopher an impress comparable, in extent and endurance, with that received more than a quarter of a century earlier amidst the memorable scenes of the first visit to Bowood. We shall see, for example, in the next chapter, how he was straightway drawn towards current politics and engaged in warfare which lasted throughout the remaining years of his life. Mill, on his side, became Bentham's favourite disciple, and wrote the history of British India under the influence of his friend's writings—an influence, says Mr. Justice Stephen, traceable in the most unmistakable manner whenever reference is made to any subject connected with law or lawyers. *History of the Criminal Law,* iii. p. 297.

CHAPTER VII BENTHAM BECOMES A POLITICIAN IN April, 1807, Grenville stoutly refused to comply with George III.'s demand for a pledge against any concession to the claims of the Catholics. The King, thereupon, expelled his Minister and dissolved Parliament. During the general election following upon the dissolution, remarkable scenes were witnessed in the City of Westminster, where a notable democratic victory was gained by Sir Francis Burdett. Grown weary of the "double imposture" of Whigs and Tories, Sir Francis had, in the preceding autumn, withdrawn from his costly struggle in Middlesex. "What' the best of kings' and 'the best of patriots' have *done for themselves"* said he, "we know and feel; what further they will *do for us* we can only conjecture."

But neither the duel between Burdett and the candidate selected to "run" with him, nor the turmoil of a fifteen days' poll, disturbed, in the slightest degree, the "hermit" of Queen's Square Place, who pursued the even tenor of his way absorbed in schemes for the reformation of the Scotch Judicature. The recluse did not, however, long maintain this attitude of indifference Cf. Wallas' *Life of Fratuis Place,* p. 44. towards current politics: a striking change was brought about, largely through the influence of

his friend James Mill, then only thirty-five years of age, and full of zeal and energy. The two men, it is true, differed greatly in disposition and mental equipment; the younger was a metaphysician, the elder was not. "Bentham, though punctilious and precise in the premises he advances," wrote Bulwer Lytton, "confines himself, in that very preciseness, to a few simple and general principles. *He seldom analyses*—he studies the human mind rather after the method of natural history than of philosophy. He enumerates—he classifies the facts—but he does not account for them." Yet Mill, despite his metaphysics, was a pronounced politician, an active and advanced Whig, a writer for the *Edinburgh* with strong views in favour of the emancipation of the Catholics; he was, moreover, eager in defence of the liberty of the Press, at that time gravely imperilled by the action of judges of the Ellenborough type. It was not long before Bentham—embittered, as some suggest, by the neglect of his Panopticon scheme—became a redoubtable protagonist of the school of Mill, wrote to Cobbett for information to be used in a "work on the subject of libel," and printed a vigorous treatise entitled, *Elements of the Art of Packing as applied to Special furies: Particularly in Cases of Libel Law.* As the book was passing through the press, the alarmed bookseller hesi *England and the English* (1833); cited in John Mill's *Early Essays,* by Gibbs, at p. 408.
"Ellenborough's eloquence," said Bentham, "is commanding: it is fierce and atrocious, the object of my abomination." Bow., v. pp. 61-186; first published 1821. tated to proceed, and suggested as a less offensive title, "Perils of the Press," while Romilly begged the author not to make it public: "I do most sincerely and anxiously entreat you not to publish it." Sir Samuel had no doubt that both the author and the printer would be prosecuted. Even a friendly attorney-general would probably have found himself under the necessity of prosecuting, from the representations which would be made to him by the judges; but Gibbs—urged Romilly—would want no such representations, and would say that not to prosecute such an attack on the whole administration of justice would be a dereliction of his duty: "Recollect what you say yourself—that it is much easier to attack King George than King Ellenboro', etc." And, indeed, the Chief Justice and his fellows were assailed in such terms that conviction would have been as certain as prosecution. Not only *money* and *power,* but *dignity* and *respect,* being secured by office, the chief object of solicitude and pursuit remaining to the judge—declared the author, in a comparatively mild passage—is *ease:* "But, so far as jury-trial is concerned, the *ease* of the *judge* is as the *obsequiousness* of the *jury.* These *volunteers,* so different from some others, being by the very nature of their situation, and without need of exertion anywhere, kept in a state of constant preparation and established discipline, waiting and wanting for nothing but the *word of command,* and drilled into that sort and degree of intelligence, which is Vicary Gibbs *(1751-1820)* was Attorney-General from 1807 to 1812. Mill, Brougham, Burdett, Miss Fox, and a few others received copies of the book, but it was not published until 1821. Letter of January 31st, 1810; Bow., x. p. 450. 'Bow., v. p. 90. sufficient for the understanding it, *labour,* on the part of the judge, is reduced to its *minimum, ease* raised to its *maximum..* . The *love of ease* is too gentle a passion to be a very active one: but what it wants in energy it makes up in extent: for there is neither *cause* nor *judicatory* in which there is not place for it. As to *vengeance,* it is only now and then, and by accident, that it comes upon the stage of judicature; but, when it does, such is its force, that, in the character of a sinister interest, no interest to the action of which that situation is ordinarily exposed can compare with it. For the exhibition of the triumphs of this tyrant passion, and of the sacrifices made to it, the *King's Bench* is, by *patent,* the great and sole *King's theatre;* the liberty of the press, its victim; *libel law,* the instrument of sacrifice."
Though Mill and Romilly were, at this period, Bentham's most intimate friends, he held intercourse with many other active politicians. Young Henry Brougham, already a prominent figure in public life, is represented as " intriguing" for invitations to dinner at the " Hermitage," and it was intended to secure for him, if possible, one of the seats at Westminster in case it should be vacated by the death of Cochrane's father. "Romilly's is the only house I go to," wrote Bentham, *1778-1868.* Contributor to *Edinburgh Review;* admitted to Lincoln's Inn 1803; M.P. for Camelford 1810; Att. Gen. to Queen Caroline; received Great Seal and a peerage 1830.
Cochrane *1775-1860)* became M.P. for Westminster 1807; convicted in 1814 of a conspiracy fraudulently to raise the price of the Funds, but he was re-elected for Westminster, and continued to sit until 1817; his father (Lord Dundonald) survived until 1831.
"and Brougham one of the very few, indeed, that I admit into mine." Both of them he regarded, at that time, as "more democratic than the Whigs." Burdett, the "hero of the mob," as Bentham dubbed him, was pressing with offers of hospitality. There was, too, correspondence with Sir James Mackintosh and Lord Holland, while Edward Sugden, afterwards Lord St. Leonards, sent a copy of his pamphlet on the Annuity Act as a " tribute due to the father of the subject."

Long manuscripts were now penned on the necessity for parliamentary reform:—" Till the time came when I had occasion to apply my mind to the present enquiry," wrote he on the 23rd January, 1810," it was blank paper on the subject.... Never having bestowed any serious thought on the subject, I never had in my own conception any tolerably correct or comprehensive view about the matter."

A *Catechism of Parliamentary Reform* was prepared, but did not appear publicly till 1817, when it was published with an Introduction of great length showing the "Necessity of Radical, and the Inadequacy of Moderate Reform." Bentham had, however, sent the Catechism, in November, 1810, to

William Cobbett, as a chapter of a proposed work on Parliamentary Reform, Cobbett being at that time editor of the *Political Register,* a journal published to revive the democratic movement, *I?8i-i &js;* Lord Chancellor 1852.

» MSS., Univ. ColL, No. 126; cited Hal., i. p. 358.

'Bow., iii. pp. 433-557. On the 23rd March, 1818, a public meeting of Westminster householders passed a resolution thanking "that profound reasoner and pre-eminent writer on Legislation, Jeremy Bentham, Esquire, for his philosophical and unanswerable vindication," etc. which had languished under the coercive laws of 1795 and 1800. The contribution was considered but, in the end, rejected by Cobbett; and this circumstance, as M. Halevy suggests, may well have constituted one cause of Bentham's pronounced and persistent antipathy towards him. *"Le philosophe politique"* described *"le politicien"* as a "vile rascal," though a "powerful writer "; as a " man filled with *odium humani generis?* Within a year of his death, while writing to a member of the Government to deprecate a proposed prosecution of Cobbett for political libel as a proceeding calculated to lower the Administration in public esteem, Bentham declared that a more odious compound of selfishness, malignity, insincerity, and mendacity had never presented itself to his memory or imagination.

A conspicuous and, occasionally, absurd figure in the politics of the time was Major Cartwright, who had advocated universal suffrage, annual parliaments, and payment of members for more than thirty years. "There is Major Cartwright," said Hazlitt, "he has but one idea or subject of discourse, Parliamentary Reform. Now, Parliamentary Reform is (as far as I know) a very good thing, a very good idea, and a very good subject to talk about; but why should it be the only one?" When he made the Major's acquaintance in 1810, Bentham was content that the franchise should be conferred on those only who paid direct taxes, but a Cf. Wallas' *Life of Place,* p. 41. Hal., ii. p. 201.

Bow., x. p. 471. June 22nd, 1831; Bow. , xi. p. 68.

Essay on *People with one Idea.*

few years later he was prepared to support a demand for universal suffrage. What principle, said he, can be more "impregnable" than universal suffrage?—" in all eyes but those to which tyranny is the only endurable form of government." The *Edinburgh Review*—in an article which, by the way, denounced the ballot as certain to deprive election of all its popular qualities and of many of its beneficial effects—asserted that his plan of reform was no other than that of Major Cartwright, "translated out of the pure and plain English which is the good Major's only valuable quality as a writer, into the peculiar language of Mr. Bentham, which his most judicious friends do not consider as his strongest point." "A great sensation," wrote Francis Place to Hodgskin in May, 1817, referring to the *Catechism* which had just appeared, " has been produced by a book in favour of universal suffrage and annual Parliaments written by Mr. Bentham." After his manner, however, the author seems to have been as much concerned to introduce reforms in procedure as to extend the right of voting beyond existing limits; he was anxious to establish a complete and regular system for the publication of parliamentary debates, and hoped, by the adoption of a secret ballot and the creation of equal electoral districts, to see the gross scandals attendant upon elections removed, or, at least, greatly reduced.

In the year 1810 Bentham placed at the disposal of James Mill the house which had been occupied by Milton; and shortly afterwards granted to his friend, at the rent of some £50, a lease of other premises overlook Vol. xxxi. p. 173. Wallas' *Life of Place,* p. *V).* ing his own garden in Queen's Square Place. During the summer months, Mill and his family were received as guests at Barrow Green, and, in later years, at Ford Abbey—a large mansion in the neighbourhood of Chard, at one time the property of Sir Edmond Prideaux, Attorney-General of the Commonwealth. Bentham became tenant of Ford Abbey in 1814, the year after his receipt of the £23,000 paid under an Act for "making compensation to Jeremy Bentham, Esquire, for the non-performance of an agreement between the said Jeremy Bentham and the Commissioners of his Majesty's Treasury, respecting the custody and maintenance of criminals." The rent asked was £800 a year, but the house, with a portion of the estate, was eventually secured for £315, subject to one month's notice to quit, with special stipulations as to the tapestry in the halls and the care of the gardens. There was, too, an altogether unnecessary provision for the preservation of the deer, which, as Bentham remarked, he was much more disposed to caress than to kill.

This magnificent abode—occupied in former days as a monastery—was situate in the midst of a beautiful and extensive park, with lakes and groves, and a noble avenue of chestnut trees stretching for more than a quarter of a mile. An imposing pile of buildings, richly ornamented, had, in the days of the Tudors, been added to the remains of the monastery, which 52 Geo. III. c. 144. About the same time Bentham acquired an interest in Robert Owen's manufacturing establishment at New Lanark, and this investment resulted in considerable pecuniary profit. (Bow., *x.* 476, 477-) were of Gothic architecture; and the whole structure (Sir Samuel Romilly tells us) presented a most striking and beautiful effect. The pleasure-grounds, gay with a vast profusion of flowers, possessed, so the tenant with rapture proclaimed, all the features of beauty imaginable, and "prodigiously" did he enjoy life there *en grand seigneur.* "I was not a little surprized," said Romilly, who visited him in the autumn of 1817, "to find in what a palace my friend was lodged. The grandeur and stateliness of the buildings, form as strange a contrast to his philosophy as the number and spaciousness of the apartments, the hall, the chapel, the corridors, and the cloisters do to the modesty and scantiness of his domestic establishment. We found him passing his time, as he always has been passing it since I have known him, which is now more than thirty years, closely applying himself, for six or eight hours a day, in writing upon laws and legislation, and in composing his Civil and Criminal Codes; and spending the remaining hours of every day in reading, or taking exercise by way of fitting himself for his labours, or, to use his own strangely invented phraseology, 'taking his ante-jentacular and post-prandial walks,' to prepare himself for his task of codification. There is something burlesque enough in this language; but it is impossible to know Bentham, and to have witnessed his benevolence, his disinterestedness, and the zeal with which he has devoted his whole life to the service of his fellow-creatures, without admiring and revering him."

Every year for four years, James Mill, with his wife and children, was entertained at Ford Abbey for about six months. Mill was up between five and six o'clock engaged on the proof-sheets of the *History of India* with the aid of his still more illustrious son—then a mere child undergoing the severe and unpleasant discipline, which made him, at the age of eight, "an adept in the first six books of Euclid and in Algebra." His father related how, during their first visit to Devonshire, the little boy had read, in addition to his Latin books, the last half of Thucydides, one play of Euripides, one of Sophocles, two of Aristophanes, and the treatise of Plutarch on education!

Bentham himself rose soon after seven, and from eight o'clock until noon was writing busily, save during a short interval for breakfast. Mill and he would sit together several hours daily, at work in a large saloon, which contained an organ and settees of the date of the Commonwealth, surrounded by cartoons beautifully executed in tapestry. At noon the host played upon the organ for an hour, occasionally engaged in a game of battledore and shuttlecock, and then, after a stroll in the fields, was at work again with his amanuensis from two o'clock until dinner at six—a simple repast without ale or wine. "The first day I came," wrote Place on August 7th, 1817, "wine was put upon the table; but, as I took none, none has since made its appearance. After dinner Mill and I take a sharp walk for two hours, say, till a quarter past eight, then one of us alternately walks with Mr. Bentham for an hour; Wallas' *Life of Place,* p. 70.
then comes tea, at which we read the periodical publications; and eleven o'clock comes but too soon, and we all go to bed." Nobody who could stay here would ever go from hence, Bentham used to say: nobody is so well anywhere else as everybody is here. In a letter written to Hodgskin during this visit to Ford Abbey, Place describes his host as "the most affable man in existence, perfectly good-humoured, bearing and forbearing, deeply read, deeply learned, eminently a reasoner, yet simple as a child; annoyed sometimes by trifles, but never by anything but trifles never worth a contentious observation."
The relations subsisting between Bentham and James Mill were of a most cordial character, and the occasions were but few when, in the language of Mill, the old man "extracted umbrage" from his behaviour. Once— it was during the first year at Ford Abbey—there was a slight break in the hitherto uninterrupted course of the friendship: perhaps they had been too much in one another's company, "which," as Mill observed in an admirable letter of explanation addressed to his host, "often makes people stale to one another, and is often fatal, without any other cause, to the happiness of the most indissoluble connexions."

The guest was very anxious to avoid an open rupture, as, on the occasion of such a quarrel, the rule of the world is to believe much of the evil which each Letter to his wife. (Wallas' *Life,* p. 76.) Place, then in his fortysixth year, was visiting the Abbey for the first time. See Mr. Wallas' interesting narrative.
Ibid., p. 81. September 19th, 1814; Bow., x. p. 481. party to the quarrel says of the other, and very little of the good each says of himself. He suggested that the long annual visit of his family should not be renewed, and hoped that this idea of limitation would give additional interest to their intercourse; "for," added he, " there is such disparity between the apparent cause —my riding out a few times in the morning with Mr. Hume to take advantage of his horses in seeing a little of the country, instead of walking with you—and the great umbrage which you have extracted, that the disposition must have been prepared by other causes and only happened first to manifest itself on that occasion. I remain with an esteem which can hardly be added to, and which, I am sure, will never be diminished, my dear Friend and Master, most affectionately yours." The coolness soon passed away; and for the greater part of the three following years Mill and his family were received as welcome guests at Ford Abbey and, indeed, formed part of the household.
Twenty-five years later an unprofitable controversy, as to the relations subsisting between the two men at this period, was excited by a reviewer in the *Edinburgh.* It arose in this wise: Bowring, in his biography which had just appeared, had indiscreetly—and probably with as little accuracy as discretion—retailed some idle words of Bentham's as to the motives which actuated Mill in framing his political creed, and further alleged that, when Bentham "took up Mill he was in great distress, and on the point of migrating to Caen." These statements were seized upon by the reviewer with much Said to be W. Empson, afterwards editor, 1847-52; vol. lxxviii. p. 460. relish and elaborated in an acrimonious essay, wherein the writer added, on his own authority, that Mill became estranged from Bentham, and "so far withdrew his allegiance from the dead lion as to deny that he had ever called him Master." John Mill, himself an Edinburgh reviewer, indignant at the publication of these and other similar allegations, obtained leave to refute them in the following number. "At the time when Bentham is said to have 'found' Mill about to 'emigrate '"—he pointed out in a concise and dignified letter —" they had already been intimate for many years, as the dates prove; since the 'emigration spoken of could not have been

projected until after the Continent was open. Like many others, Mr. Mill had thoughts of removing to a country where a small income would go further in supporting and educating a family; but a person is not usually said to be 'in great distress' who never in his life was in debt, and whose income, whatever it might be, always covered his expenses." Bentham and Mill had, indeed, formed a scheme of migrating together to Venezuela, which, according to Bentham, was a land abundantly watered both by rains and rivers, with a delightful summer temperature all the year round: "Within sight of the sea, though almost under the line, you have a mountain topped with ice, so that you may absolutely choose your temperature, and enjoy the vegetable luxuries of all countries." Nor was there any real basis for the suggestion of *estrangement:* after Mill's appointment to the India House in the summer of 1819, the inter Bow., x. p. 457.
course between him and Bentham was, no doubt, less frequent, but it is beyond question that their friendship continued unimpaired throughout the life of the elder man. John Mill declared that his father's feeling towards his old friend never changed; nor did he ever fail, publicly or privately, in giving due honour to Bentham's name, or in acknowledgment of the intellectual debt he owed to him: "The 'allegiance' which he disclaimed was only that which no man, who thinks for himself, will own to another. He was no otherwise a disciple of Bentham, than of Hobbes, Hartley, or Ricardo."2
On September 13th, 1818, James Mill himself wrote: "It is really a source of happiness to myself to be near him *(i. e.* Bentham), and though there are no small incompatibilities between us, I could not part from him without a good deal of emotion. The union in intellectuals is perfect, which, with the first man in intellectuals of his age, cannot fail to be a source of pleasure; and in the morals and sympathies, with a good many clashings between him and me, there is also much in his character to love, his sincerity and simplicity of character it would not be easy to match, and there is nothing which goes so far as these two qualities in laying the foundation of attachment."

The mention of Ricardo serves to recall the fact that he was a visitor both at Ford Abbey and the Hermitage, but Bentham describes him as the *disciple* rather Cf., *e.g.,* Bentham's letter to Chamberlain Clarke, August, 1828. *Ibid.,* p. 605. *Early Essays,* by Gibbs, at p. 414. » MSS. cited Hal., ii. pp. 374-5.
than the *master* of James Mill: "Mill was the spiritual father of Ricardo," he used to say, "while I am the spiritual father of Mill," thus claiming the economist as "a sort of spiritual grandson. " Mill, says M. Hal6vy, was the man of action who supplied, to some extent, will-power to the cautious and hesitating Ricardo.
So early as 1793 Bentham had himself written a long essay on "Political Economy," some portions of which appeared in *Bibliotheque Brittanique* for 1798. The essay itself was sent by Dumont to Speranski, the Russian statesman and reformer, who, in a letter dated October 10th, 1804, wrote: "I believe that in following the Plan of Mr. Bentham Political Economy would occupy a position much more natural, more easily to be studied, and more scientific. You may thus judge the value I attach to the promised work." But there was really very little that was novel in Bentham's speculations, and, after the preparation of this manuscript, he abandoned the pursuit of the subject, except in so far as its study was necessarily involved in that of the science of legislation. Accepting many of the conclusions of Adam Smith, whose genius he greatly admired, Bentham examined the problems of Political Economy with special reference to the laws that should govern a nation's commerce and regulate its industries. Rigorously confining himself to questions of immediate practical importance—such as the problems of population and finance—he declared what ought to be done, and, above all, what ought not to be done, with a view Hal., ii. p. 217.
Bow., iii. p. 73 n. The chapter on " Population " so appeared. to the advancement of national prosperity. He founded his arguments upon the principle that production and trade are limited by the amount of capital in a country; and, reasoning on this as a sole and sufficient basis, he affirmed that *security* and *freedom* is all that industry requires for its complete development. He urged the necessity for the removal of national jealousies, and sought to combat the overweening desire for colonial expansion—the promotion of colonisation, not as a mode of relieving population, but in the hope of enriching the mother country. We should, he maintained, cease to consider colonies with the "greedy eyes of fiscality": "If wisdom alone were listened to, the ordinary object of contention would be reversed—the mother country would desire to see her children powerful that they might become free, and the colonies would fear the loss of that tutelary authority which gave them internal tranquillity and security against external foes."1
To destroy foreign commerce, it is only necessary to sell everything and purchase nothing: such (said he) is the folly which has been passed off as the depth of political wisdom among statesmen. Trade has been confounded with gambling, in which the gain of one man is always founded upon the loss of another—it has been pretended that men can only enrich themselves by despoiling others, that they live as gladiators only by destroying one another. On the contrary, in a social undertaking all the adventurers may reap their share of advantage; since, other things being equal, Bow., iii. p. 57.
the more labour there is, the greater will be the result. Agriculture, manufactures, commerce have no need of favour, they demand only a secure and open road.

These manuscripts on Political Economy were eventually made use of by Dumont in the *Tk/orie des Peines et des Recompenses,* the first edition of which was published at Paris in 1811. The second volume of that work was rendered into English, and appeared, in 1825, under the title of *Rationale of Reward?* It was edited by Richard Smith, of the

Stamps and Taxes, who prepared for the press many of Bentham's MSS. In Bowring's edition, however, Book IV. of the *Rationale of Reward i.e.* the portion relating to Political Economy) was re-edited from the original MSS., and appeared separately under the title of *A Manual of Political Economy?* Bentham proposed, amongst other measures, the creation of prizes for the encouragement of discoveries and research, and the institution of a Register of Trade Marks. He advocated, also, the free grant of Patents—then charged with exorbitant fees—or, at least, that no fees should be paid until the inventor had reaped some benefit from the Patent.

As we have already seen, the *Tactiques des Assembl/es d/libe'rantes* and the *Traite des Sophismes politiques, etc.* , were published at Geneva in 1816; and in that and the following years there appeared two octavo volumes entitled *Chrestomathia, or Useful Education,* a curious and uninviting collection of papers explanatory of the design of an institution " proposed to be set on foot under the Bow., ii. pp. 189-266; and cf. iii. pp. 31-84.

Bow., iii. pp. 31-84.

name of the Chrestomathic day school for the extension of the new system of instruction to the higher branches of learning." Mill, Place, Wakefield, and others interested in a scheme for the extension of the Lancasterian system to Secondary Education having secured his support, Bentham, it seems, not only wrote commending the system of education as based on utilitarian principles, but even offered his garden as a site for the erection of a school. The building plan, however, presented great objections, which led him gradually to impose harder and harder conditions; and in 1820, says Mr. Wallas, "after an enormous correspondence, his offer of a site was finally declined, and the project was given up." It was during this period that Bentham wrote the lengthy manuscripts on educational subjects, which are published by Bowring in his eighth volume under the titles: *A Fragment on Ontology, Essay on Logic, Essay on Language, Fragments on Universal Grammar."*

In the year 1817 he published a tract written to expose the mischief arising from the laws relating to the administration of oaths; it was entitled *Swear not at all* and had been printed originally in 1813. In Bow., viii. pp. 1-191; Place saw this work through the press. The actual curriculum proposed for the higher Lancasterian schools was largely borrowed from it. (Wallas' *Life of Place,* pp. 84, lot.) *Life of Place,* p. 112.

Bow., viii. pp. 193-357. These papers are justly described by Halevy as *"les longs et inutiles manuscrits"* (it p. 357).

Bow., v. pp. 187-229; and c£ *ibid.,* ii. p. 210, and *ibid.,* vi. and vii. *passim.* See now 6 *6 Will. 4, c. 62* and the Oaths Act of 1888 *Ji* cV *J2 Vict. c. 46),* etc. Bentham recommended that courts should be fitted up with a picture of Ananias and Sapphira. some cases, so he declared, the Promissory Oath prevented a man from doing what he knew to be right; in others, it afforded him a ready excuse for the commission of some wrong. George III. laid on his Coronation Oath the responsibility of the American War and of his resistance to the claims of the Catholics. He had sworn to maintain his dominions entire; he had sworn to preserve the Church of England. At Oxford, barbers, cooks, bedmakers, errand boys, and other unlettered retainers to the University were habitually sworn in English to the observance of a medley of statutes penned in Latin—the oath thus solemnly taken being never kept. On matriculating, he had himself been excused from taking the oaths by reason of his tender years; and this, said Bowring, relieved him from a state of very painful doubt, for even then he felt strong objections against needless swearing. At a later period of his University career, when called upon to subscribe the Thirty-nine Articles, he experienced great "distress of mind," for in some parts of that " dogmatical formulary " he found no meaning at all; in others, no meaning save one, which, in his eyes, was "but too plainly irreconcileable either to reason or to scripture." It is probable that he had not so much as heard of the conven ient doctrine of *non-natural interpretation* in vogue eighty years afterwards.

Bentham did not, however, regard Assertory or Judicial Oaths as open to the same serious objections; but, while recognising the necessity of some formal sanction, he did not approve of the ceremony being made a sacred invocation, for that was apt to obscure the real mischief of judicial falsehood—the mischief occasioned by the lie. If criminality be centred in the profanation of the ceremony, who is to say whether the sanction for truth be in operation or not? Who can say what are the religious opinions hidden in the breast of the witness? First went ordeal, he writes; then went duel; after that went, under the name of wager of law, the ceremony of an oath in its pure state; by-and-by this last of the train of supernatural powers, *ultima coelicolum,* will be gathered with Astrsa into its native skies.

In February, 1818, Henry Bickersteth—the distinguished equity lawyer who in after years became Lord Langdale—being an ardent advocate of parliamentary reform, was bent on inducing the authors of various rival schemes to concentrate upon one definite plan, to be propounded by Bentham and proclaimed by Burdett. "If," said he, " the names of Bentham and Burdett went together in this proceeding, we should not only have universal notoriety, but all the reflection and sagacity, as well as all the active zeal in the kingdom, would be called into immediate action on this subject." Reform, he declared, could be peaceably obtained only by the pressure of public opinion, acting with continually increasing uniformity and weight in favour of the cause; and in such matters public opinion is, he affirmed, no more than the opinion of some individual, so advantageously promulgated and so well sustained *1783-1851.* Senior Wrangler 1808, called to the Bar 1811. In 1836 he succeeded Lord Cottenham as Master of the Rolls. Bow., x. p. 493. that it is in the end adopted by the multitude as their own.

Burdett was well content to play the

rdle assigned to him; but Bentham protested that, for his part, he was quite unprepared to cope with the necessary details, and felt a diffidence of his own strength, such as, he must confess, was not generally accounted among the number of his weaknesses. These scruples were, however, overcome; and at Bickersteth's suggestion, he drew up a series of concise and forcible resolutions, which, while setting forth the principal abuses complained of, embodied "the more general regulations constituting the intended remedy." Burdett undertook to move the resolutions: "My tongue shall speak," said he, " as you do prompt mine ear.... My first reward will be the hope of doing everlasting good to my country; my next, and only inferior to it, that of having my name linked in immortality with that of Jeremy Bentham; and though, to be sure, it is but as a tomtit mounted on an eagle's wing, the thought delights me. Bentham and Burdett!—the alliteration charms my ear."

Sir Francis did not approve of adding to the demand for universal suffrage and annual Parliaments any declaration in favour of the Ballot, fearing that its introduction would create great prejudice against the scheme; but the draughtsman insisted upon secret voting as fundamental, and the resolutions were moved, as a whole, on the 2nd June, 1818. In these resolutions, remarks M. Halevy, the principle of the artificial identification of interests, *entre les gouvernants et les gouvernds,* was rigorously applied, though in conformity with the traditional spirit of the English Constitution. But the proposals received no support whatsoever either from the Tories or from the Whigs, and were got rid of by a motion for the order of the day. Canning spoke for the Tories; and Brougham, rising from the Whig benches, while declaring his profound respect for Bentham—a man, said he, removed from the turmoil of active life, who had voluntarily abandoned the emoluments and the power which it holds out to dazzle ambitious and worldly minds—denounced the schemes of the member for Westminster as chimerical and visionary. He sneered at the Ballot and ridiculed Burdett's proposals for the extension of the suffrage; they were not, indeed, said he, so consistent as those of that more sturdy reformer, Bentham, who would not admit of a line being drawn even at the gates of Bedlam, who tossed away the rule and scale altogether. Young or old, men or women, sane or insane, all must vote; all must have a voice in electing their representative.

Burdett replied with much eloquence to this attempt "to render ridiculous the ablest advocate which Reform had ever found—the illustrious and unrivalled Bentham." And, in truth, Brougham greatly overstated his case. Bentham, in his plan of Parliamentary Reform, had expressly excluded minors and persons unable to read. It is true that he forbore from excluding the insane in terms; and that he was disposed to extend the suffrage to women, though he recognised that the public was not, as yet, prepared for so great an innovation. He could not discover any reason for the exclusion of females, and he pointed out that those, who in support

N of it gave a sneer or a laugh for a reason because they could not find a better, had no objection to the vesting of absolute power in that sex and in a single hand. It is, however, interesting to note that, in the unpublished essay on *Representation,* written in 1789 *ante,* p. 98), Bentham had stated very tersely the grounds for refusing the franchise to married women. In the same essay he had, in terms, recognised the incapacity of the insane; but, in preparing his plan of reform, he treated their exclusion as a matter of small importance and as likely to give birth to disputes and litigation.

Shortly after the rejection of Sir Francis Burdett's motion, Parliament was dissolved, and a requisition was presented to Romilly inviting him to become a candidate for the City of Westminster. Sir Samuel complied with the requisition, and a fierce contest ensued. Bentham did not vote, but, for the first and last time in his life, took active part in an electoral struggle by writing a hand-bill—on behalf of Burdett and Douglas Kinnaird, the Radical candidates—against his old friend Romilly, who had become, in Bentham's phrase, " no better than a Whig." Romilly was returned at the head of the poll, yet never took his seat for Westminster, dying by his own hand on the first day of Michaelmas term in the same year, his wife, to whom he was most tenderly attached, having died but three days before. Worn by sleepless nights during the long weeks of Lady Romilly's illness, distraught by an anxiety which culminated in despair, his mind gave way under the strain, and his useful life was brought to a close in the sixtysecond year of his age.

The sad death of his dear and constant associate was severely felt by Bentham, but the gentle Romilly had happily not allowed the incidents of the election to interfere in any way with their personal relations. Three weeks after the contest we find him dining with his " most excellent friend "—" a small but very pleasant party"—and almost the last page of his diary records that, while some of his acquaintances were very angry with Bentham for his hostile interference, he himself felt not the least resentment. "Though a late I know him to be a very sincere convert to the expediency of Universal Suffrage," wrote Romilly, "and he is too honest in his politics to suffer them to be influenced by any considerations of private friendship." *Memoirs,* iii. p. 365.

CHAPTER VIII BENTHAM IN OLD AGE

WHEN Bentham, in 1818, determined his tenancy of Ford Abbey—owing, it is said, to the loss of some 8,000, recently adventured in a Devonshire marble mine, which had been acquired by a man "who had a patent of some sort and went out of his mind "— he retired to the house in Queen's Square Place, and during the remaining years of his life rarely left its precincts. This dwelling is described by Rush, the American Minister, as "a peculiar place of residence, unique and romantic-like," situate at the end of a kind of blind alley which widened into a small neat courtyard—"shrubbery graced its area, and flowers its window-sills—it was like an oasis in the desert—its name the' Hermitage.

'" Inside the house Rush found everything prim and orderly, the furniture, indeed, seemed to have stood unmoved for generations. A parlour, library, and dining-room made up the suite of apartments, each of which contained a piano, "the eccentric master of the whole being fond of music as the recreation of his literary hours." The garden, dark with the shade of ancient trees which formed a barrier *Residence at the Court of London,* p. 286. against all intrusion, had once been distinguished for its variety of fruits; but at the beginning of the nineteenth century a few currants and gooseberries, with abundance of fine mulberries, were all that time and smoke had left.
The "hermit," as he called himself, wrote on an average from ten to fifteen folio pages a day, and, in later years, every page was headed with the date of its composition. If, while occupied with one subject, something worth remembering occurred to him on another, he forthwith noted it on a slip of paper, which was pinned to a small green curtain hanging near; and his disciples would sometimes find the curtain covered with such memoranda. He took the air in his garden with great regularity, walking, or rather trotting, as if impatient for exercise: in addition to " antejentacular " and " postprandial" perambulations, he enjoyed an " ante-prandial circumgyration." It has been said that you would be as sure of finding him at home as of finding Robinson Crusoe in his island—his white hair, long and flowing; his neck bare; dressed in a brown, quaker-cut coat, light brown cassimere breeches, list shoes, and white worsted stockings drawn over his breeches' knees—in general appearance strikingly like Benjamin Franklin, though of a more benign and cheerful cast of countenance. For his years he seemed remarkably hale and vigorous, but his eyes were dim and his rest much disturbed by dreams and extreme physical sensibility. If his hand touched his body, it is said that he at once awoke in pain.

The peaceful routine of life in his pleasant home is thus described by Bentham in a letter to one W. Thompson, of Cork, who had consulted him as to the possibility of establishing a Chrestomathic school in that city: "During your stay in London, my hermitage, such as it is, is at your service.... I am a single man, turned of seventy; but as far from melancholy as a man need be. Hour of dinner, six; tea, between nine and ten; bed, a quarter before eleven. Dinner and tea in society; breakfast, my guests, whoever they are, have at their own hour, and by themselves; my breakfast, of which a newspaper, read to me to save my weak eyes, forms an indispensable part, I take by myself. Wine I drink none, being in that particular, of the persuasion of Jonadab, the son of Rechab. At dinner, soup, as constantly as if I were a Frenchman, an article of my religion learned in France; meat, one or two sorts, as it may happen; ditto, sweet things of which, with the soup, the principal part of my dinner is composed. Of the dessert, the frugality matching with that of the dinner. Coffee for anyone that chooses it."

In extreme age he seems to have accustomed himself to take a small quantity of wine—some half glass of Madeira daily.

During these years of retirement in the Hermitage, Bentham kept in close touch with men who were active and prominent in the outer world; with Brougham, in particular, to whom he supplied much political material, or "pap," as the future Chancellor called it, he was in constant communication. "Insincere as Brougham is" —so he is reported to have said—" it is always worth my while to bestow a day on him. I am going off the stage, he keeps on." "Dear Grandpapa," wrote the great advocate in 1827, " many thanks for the *pap,* I am already *fat on it.* I did not acknowledge it, being busy eating it; and saying nothing at meals is the way with us little ones—when hungry. I shall be in town next week late. Yours dutifully. " The old man, who specially approved Brougham's efforts in favour of popular education, and was, we are told, much delighted with his phrase, "the schoolmaster is abroad," at once replied, begging his " dear sweet little poppet" to toddle to the Hermitage immediately on its return to receive more "pap made in the same saucepan." But the "little poppet" proved a great disappointment to Bentham—the wisdom of the reformer could not, he said, "overcome the craft of the lawyer." Worse even than his persistent opposition to the Ballot was his half-hearted attempt to reform the entanglements and technicalities of law proceedings: "Brougham's mountain is delivered, and behold!—the mouse." Many of Peel's projects are merely for the creation of new offices with large salaries, said Bentham one day to Bowring; the places fail, but the salaries have to be paid, and so there comes a cry against reform. Brougham, with his support of special pleading, is, he declared, as bad as Peel—" boys of the same school, heirs of the same inheritance, preachers of the same faith! Shake them in a bag: look at them playing push-pin together!"

In March, 1830, Bentham refused "pap" to the Bentham cites the phrase as, "the schoolmaster is seut abroad." (Bow., v. p. 609

"naughty, naughty boy," Master Henry Brougham, who had outgrown it. "What you are in want of is another dose of jalap to purge off your bad humours, and a touch, every now and then, of the tickle Toby which I keep in pickle for you." Master Peel was now, by comparison, a real good boy—growing better and better every day—from whom a lesson should be taken. No more law-fees for him, no more cramming of his playfellows with them, so the nice " Parliament gingerbread " shall be given to *him* to munch.

In 1831 Brougham had become Lord Chancellor; and Bentham, within a few months of his death, wrote an attack on the Chancellor's proposal to absorb, in his own Court, the Courts of the Vice-Chancellor and of the Master of the Rolls. This article, with some elaborate and, indeed, carping criticisms of the Bankruptcy Court Bill, was published in 1832, under the title, *Lord Brougham Displayed* While describing the Chancellor as one of the most admirable

members this country ever saw of the most highly talented profession, and as a most amiable man in private life, Bentham did not hesitate to charge him with a greed for patronage, nor scruple to refer to him as the lord high jobber driving on his course with his learned job horses, contemplating a fall upon his bed of down—the retiring pension. Brougham affirmed that his Bill would result in a great diminution of the patronage and advantages then belonging to the Keeper of the Great Seal, and with much forbearance spoke admiringly of the critic, who had thus impugned his motives, as "a personal Bow., v. pp. 549-612.
friend of mine—a man of extraordinary learning, the father of the English Bar, and the father of law reform."

John Cam Hobhouse, the companion and friend of Lord Byron, was, at this period, Burdett's colleague in the representation of Westminster. He frequently visited Bentham, and undertook to arrange some of his manuscripts and put his words into the vernacular; "although I suspect," said he, "it would be difficult to find language more to the purpose than Bentham's own." He expressed, in particular, a wish to edit the manuscripts on Political Fallacies; but they were, in fact, edited by one Bingham, with assistance from Place and James Mill, and published in 1824. The *Book of Fallacies* consists of a laborious, but incisive, exposure of many mischievous absurdities which passed current as good sense in political assemblies; and it was directed mainly against the devices made use of in support of corruption and arbitrary power. Thus Bentham ridicules appeals to the Wisdom of our Ancestors, "the Chinese Argument"; the Hobgoblin Argument, "No Innovation!"; the Procrastinator's Argument, "Wait a little, this is not the time "; the Snail's Pace Argument, " One thing at a time!" " Not so fast!" "Slow and Sure!" and so on. Fallacies of " Confusion " are also admirably dealt with; for example, the use of " impostor terms" applied to the defence of things which under their proper name are manifestly indefensible, as where a man, delighted Afterwards Lord Broughton (1786-1869).
Wallas' *Life of Place,* p. 83.
Bow., ii., pp. 375-488; see Dumont's *Sophistries Politique.* to be supposed " a man of gallantry," would be far from pleased if he were plainly designated "an adulterer." Sydney Smith, who declared that he read everything its author wrote, reviewed the book in the *Edinburgh* stating his conviction that most persons would prefer to become acquainted with Mr. Bentham through the medium of reviews, " after that eminent philosopher has been washed, trimmed, shaved, and forced into clean linen." The chief fallacies, so happily exposed by Bentham, are gathered together by his reviewer in the well-known "Noodle's Oration," beginning: "What would our ancestors say to this, Sir? How does this measure tally with their institutions? How does it agree with their experience? Are we to put the wisdom of yesterday in competition with the wisdom of centuries? *Hear, hear.)* Is beardless youth to show no respect for the decisions of mature age? (Loud cries of *hear, hear.)* If this measure be right, would it have escaped the wisdom of those Saxon progenitors to whom we are indebted for so many of our best political institutions? Would the Danes have passed it over? Would the Normans have rejected it?" It is from the folly, not from the wisdom, of our ancestors, said Bentham, that we have so much to learn; experience, indeed, is the very mother of wisdom.

Many strange rumours as to the old man's singularities obtained currency in those days both here and in the United States. Most of them were highly coloured, and some of them wholly false. *The Times* actually published a letter stating that, having invited August, 1825.
one Parry to breakfast and dine with him, he gave his guest no breakfast at all and left him without dinner until ten o'clock at night. The writer of the letter, presumably Parry himself—an engineer who worked under the inventor of the Congreve rockets— added that, as they walked in the public streets, the appearance of his host was so ridiculous as to bring upon them the ribald insults of a notorious strumpet.

Bentham's conduct was, in truth, sufficiently peculiar to afford some ground for such reports. No disturbance of the regular routine was allowed, even for a moment; he refused to receive his old acquaintance, Lovell Edgeworth, and would not return calls paid to him by the Duke of Richmond and Lord Sydney. Madame de Stael applied to Dumont for an introduction, saying, "Tell Bentham I will see nobody till I have seen him." "Sorry for it," grumbled Bentham, "for then she will never see anybody." We can, however, hardly assign this refusal to admit the famous authoress in his house solely to anxiety lest his thoughts should be distracted, for he was in the habit, we are told, of referring to her, in conversation, as a " trumpery magpie."

The strict seclusion of the Hermitage probably served to intensify the bashfulness which, according to the hermit's account, clung to him like a cold garment through life. But he often proved himself "on hospitable thoughts intent," and the guests found a dinner daintily served when Anne, the housemaid, summoned them to "the Shop," as Bentham called the room where he dined. It was surrounded by books, and contained an organ which was played while the party sat down to dinner. The table was always liberally supplied, and he delighted to devise means of giving pleasure to his guests: if he chanced to discover that one of them specially relished any particular dish, it was prepared and quietly placed before him. "Get together a gang," he wrote to Brougham in May, 1822, "and bring them to the Hermitage, to devour such eatables and drinkables as are to be found in it." "From Honourable House," Brougham was directed to bring Denman— Queen Caroline's Solicitor-General, afterwards to become Lord Chief Justice—Joseph Hume, Sir James Mackintosh, and David Ricardo; from the India House he was to bid James Mill—" Hour of attack, half past six; Hour of commencement of plunderage, seven; Hour of expulsion—with the aid of the adjacent Police Office if necessary—quarter before eleven; Day of attack to be determined by Universal Suffrage. N.B. to be performed with advantage all plunderage must be regulated.... Witness; Matchless Constitution."

At the age of eighty he wrote to Burdett: "Francis, I see how it is with you. You don't know where to go for a dinner; and so you are coming to me. I hear that you have been idler than usual, since you were in my service; always running after the hounds, whenever you could get anybody to trust you with a horse. I hear you are got among the Tories, and that you said once you were one of them; you must have been in your cups. You had been reading *High Life below Stairs,* I suppose, and wanted them to call you Lord Burdett.
Cf. Bow., xi. p. 38, where Bentham states that he had but one interview with Denman, for whom, however, he felt "esteem and affection."
You have always had a hankering after bad company whatever I could do to keep you out of it."

After Bentham's death, Sir Francis did, indeed, "get among the Tories"; for, in 1837, at the age of sixtyseven, he retired from the representation of Westminster, and was returned as a Conservative for North Wiltshire.

When no guests were expected, the old man dined with one of his secretaries, whom he called "reprobate"; sometimes two " reprobates " would share his meal. He keenly appreciated the pleasures of the table; though during the last few years of his life, the sense of taste was much impaired, and he formed the habit of beginning dinner with dessert, declaring that he wholly lost the flavour of the fruit if he ate it after stronger viands.

At eleven o'clock his nightcap was brought in, his watch handed over to the "reprobate" who held for the time being the office of "putter to bed," his eyes washed, and his clothes removed; he was then "read to sleep" by one of the "reprobates," each of whom had sworn fealty to a *trinoda necessitas,* the asportation of the candle, the "transtration" of the window, " item of the trap-window."

It was in 1820 that Bentham formed the acquaintance of his biographer, John Bowring, who was then about twenty-eight years of age. Bowring was introduced to the old man's notice by a naval offlcer named Blaquiere—" a sort of wandering apostle of Bentham Author of *Letters from the Mediterranean* (1813) and *History of the Revolution in Spain* (1822. He was an active member of the Greek Committee with which Bentham associated himself in 1823-4. A boat, in which he embarked at Plymouth for the Azores, was lost at sea.
ism"—as one possessing a special knowledge of the Spanish Peninsula; and, as the first fruits of the connection, there appeared in the following year letters addressed to the Spanish People on " *the Liberty of the Press & Public Discussion"* and a volume containing the *Three Tracts relative to Spanish and Portuguese affairs, with a continual eye to English ones:* (a) *On a House of Lords,* (b) *On fudicial Delays,* (c) *On Antiquated Constitutions? A* close intimacy sprang up, and the younger man was always a welcome guest at the Hermitage; frequently he became an inmate of the house, and received, he tells us, at the hands of his host, blessings, benefits, benignities, courtesies in every shape. The most interesting portion of his correspondence was placed by Bentham in Bowring's hands; and he bequeathed all his manuscripts to Bowring's care, in order that he might superintend their publication. A fairly complete edition of the works appeared in 1843; but the letters and memoirs are ill-digested and badly arranged.
The old man's friendship, so Bowring declares, was to him that of a guardian angel: "It conducted me, with faithful devotion, through a period of my existence in which I was steeped in poverty and overwhelmed with slander. His house was an asylum—his purse a treasury—his heart an Eden—his mind a fortress to me. It is only since his death, and when, in my situation of executor, all his papers have fallen into my hands, that I have learned how much I owed to his courageous friendship—his unbroken, his unbending trust."

When the *Westminster Review* was started in 1823 Bow., ii. pp. 75-97-Bow., viiL pp. 463-86.
the necessary funds were provided by Bentham. The Whigs being already represented by the *Edinburgh,* and the Tories by the *Quarterly,* the new periodical was projected as an organ of the Radicals. Bowring at first managed the political department; and the important section known as the "Reviewers Reviewed" was supplied by James Mill, who opened with a trenchant attack on the *Edinburgh* as the older of the two existing papers. Afterwards the whole control fell for a time into the hands of Bowring; but he was by no means well fitted for editorial work, and in later years, the responsibility was shared by that able man and accomplished writer, Colonel Perronet Thompson. Reform, as Sir Leslie Stephen says, was now becoming respectable, and even the Whigs were gaining courage to take it up seriously. In October, 1826, Bentham himself contributed—in an ingenious and suggestive review of Humphrey's important proposals for a Real Property Code—some criticisms, which doubtless had a direct influence on the land law reforms of 1832 and 1833. The review is written throughout in a crabbed and perplexing style; for, while denouncing "surplusage" and "involvedness" as the efficient causes of the " lengthiness" of conveyancing instruments, the writer seems to have had no perception of the beam in his own eye. Place at first refused to contribute to the new magazine unless his articles were published without alteration. "Mine must be legitimate children," he wrote, "however Bow., v. pp. 387-416.
In July, 1831, Bentham forwarded to the Commissioners appointed to inquire into the Law of Real Property an elaborate outline of a *Plan for a General Register of Real Property.* ugly and ungraceful they may be." No! characteristically observed Bentham to the editor, "*ugly or ungraceful* children we cannot adopt, nor will we traffic in *pigs in a poke"*
The two tracts known as the *Defences of Economy against Burke and Rose—*

written in 1810 and first published in 1817—were republished during the year 1830 in a volume entitled *Official Aptitude Maximised: Expense Minimised?* which also contained reprints of *Observations on Mr. Secretary Peel's Speech on the Police Magistrates Bill* and of the famous *Indications respecting Lord Eldon.* The "Indications," originally published in 1824, had been sent to the press in spite of urgent representations by the author's legal friends, who declared that prosecution and conviction would assuredly follow the publication of this philippic. John Scott (1751-1838), Earl of Eldon, had held the Seals for more than twenty years, and the state of business in his Court of Chancery had, in the words of Romilly, then, perhaps, the ablest counsel at the bar, long been a most grievous and intolerable evil to the suitors. Though neither eloquent nor accomplished, Eldon was a man of powerful understanding, with a profound knowledge of case law, and during his short reign in the Common Pleas, had proved himself to be endowed with many judicial qualities of a high order: sitting in Banc he was *bound* to keep pace with his fellows; sitting with a jury he was *bound* to resolve forthwith the questions raised for his ruling. In the Court of Chancery, however, his indecision and habits of pro Wallas' *Life of Place,* p. 87. Bow., v. pp. 263-386.

crastination soon occasioned serious delays, and the scandal was more than once brought before the notice of Parliament. But at the time Bentham wrote, arrears of undecided causes, motions, and petitions were still growing apace, and the unhappy suitors "dragged at each remove a lengthening chain." His scathing indictment was not, however, directed only against Eldon's dilatory methods; it was levelled also against certain gross abuses which prevailed both in the Chancery and King's Bench offices—fees exacted for services never performed, valuable sinecures created by a gradual and insidious process, the irregular attendances of the higher officials in receipt of very large incomes, a system of gratuities constantly augmented, which, as Sir James Mansfield well said, was the very mother of extortion. Years before, a solicitor of standing called Lowe had complained, by way of petition, against the " corruption of office"; and, in particular, had charged the illegal exaction of specific sums claimed as fees due to the secretary of bankrupts. Now these fees, in fact, formed part of the Chancellor's emoluments, and it is known that in one year he received from this source alone £4,900; accordingly, Eldon desired the Master of the Rolls to assist him on the hearing of the petition, and managed to extricate himself from this delicate position by a characteristic expedient. After argument the Court took time to consider judgment—but, says Romilly, who was one of the counsel engaged, *no judgment was ever given, and the fees were taken by the Lord Chancellor as before.* An instructive chapter of Bentham's pamphlet, dealing with another illegal exaction, is headed: "How the illegality got wind and how Felix trembled!" Lord Eldon, he says, advised His Majesty to commission Lord Eldon to report upon the conduct of Lord Eldon, and the title of the next chapter tells its own tale: "How the Chancellor went to Parliament and got corruption established." /On 28th June, 1825, Eldon defended himself before a sympathetic audience in the House of Lords, closing his speech with a reference to his favourite topic—the purity of his own conscience. "I am incorrupt in office; and I can form no better wish for my country than that my successor shall be penetrated with an equal desire to execute his duties with fidelity." Many years before, in his speech as Attorney-General against Horne Tooke, he had, after his manner, justified his own character: "It is the little inheritance I have to leave to my children, and, by God's help, I will leave it unimpaired." Here he shed tears, and to the astonishment of the Court, the Solicitor-General—Mitford, afterwards Lord Redesdale—began to weep in concert. "Just look at Mitford," said a bystander to Home Tooke: "What on earth is *he* crying for?" "He is crying," placidly replied the accused, " to think of the *little* inheritance Scott's children are likely to get." /

In acknowledging a presentation copy of *Official Aptitude Maximised,* Sir James Graham (1792-1861) wrote to Bentham: "Permit me to offer my sincere thanks for the present of your valuable work, which I shall study with the respect due to the production of the most enlightened and honest jurist, every mark *Edin. Rev.,* vol. lxxxi. p. 170.

of whose approbation is regarded by me as an honourable distinction." It was in this same year (1830) that Graham brought forward his memorable motion for the reduction of official salaries.

Bentham's *Radical Reform Bill* had been published in December, 1819, and the tract, *Radicalism not Dangerous2* was written about the same date, though never published in the author's lifetime. In 1822 a small octavo appeared, bearing the motto "Leave us alone," and entitled: *Observations on the Restrictive and Prohibitory Commercial System, especially with a reference to the decree of the Spanish Cortes ofJuly, 1S20.* This little volume, which contains a forcible exposition of the principles of Free Trade and the dangers of Retaliation, was edited by Bowring, who some years earlier had been sent to Spain and Portugal as the representative of a commercial house. In most cases, says the author, the prohibitory system produces a retaliatory operation, and the power of retaliation possessed against a nation is often very great. What, he asks, will be the condition of a state, if other countries, whose wares are excluded, load with excessive taxation, or exclude by total prohibition, the surplus of her produce for which she has no consumption at home? It cannot fail to be calamitous—and even should ill-will be averted from a sense that no injury was intended, contempt will occupy its place in proportion as the impolicy of the system is manifest.

Though far removed from the "levellers" and "com Bow., iii. pp. 558-97. *Ibid.,* pp. 599-622.

Ibid., pp. 85-103. munists," Bentham

deeply distrusted the Whigs, and would have no fellowship with the "canny" opportunism which fashioned the politics of such men as Henry Brougham.

He was, indeed, rapidly becoming—if he had not already become—the oracle of the Radicals, the recognised Master of a School of advanced Politicians. *Parle fait mime que Bentham devient radical, le parti radical va changer de caractere,* says M. Halevy; and, in truth, although he was now an ardent reformer and determined champion of Liberty, a convinced republican and opponent of a "Second Chamber," there was nothing of the Revolutionary or Jacobin about the new leader. Two years before his death, in a memorandum of "J. B.'s Creed," he declared his preference for the English Constitution—"such as it is"—to non-government, and, indeed, to every other but the United States Government. "But I do not prefer it," he continued, "such as it is, teeming with abuses and other imperfections, to what it would be if cleared, in the whole or part, of all or any of these same imperfections." Writing in 1822, he described the English Government as the least bad of all bad governments, that of the United States as the first of all governments to which the epithet *good,* in the positive sense of the word, could with propriety be applied.

Although a severe critic of the laws of entail and Vol. ii. p. 212; cf. Redlich and Hirst's *English Local Government,* i. p. 96.

See his Letter to his Fellow Citizens of France, which converted O'Connell to the anti-Second Chamber faith. (Bow., iv. pp. 419-50, and ix. p. 144.) of the principle which favours the accumulation of property in the hands of one member of the family, he fully recognised the necessity for assuring men in the enjoyment of their wealth. The treasure of the comparatively rich is—as he well said—an insurance office to the comparatively indigent; but security must be given to its owners, and the demands made upon them, by way of provision for the poor, must be so regulated as not to afford an inducement to idleness in those who claim relief from their wealthier neighbours. He insisted, however, that the property of the rich is in no real danger from the poor; while the property of the poor is not only in danger from the rich, but constantly encroached on by them. "The small property of the poor is, every particle of it, necessary to their subsistence: it is, therefore, more carefully watched and guarded.... But the property of the poor is of no value in the eyes of the rich: hence they conclude it to be of little value in the eyes of its possessors." He was of opinion that the tyranny of the rich over the poor would exist, to an appreciable extent, even in the most perfect democracy; but equality in respect of legal power would—so he believed—be sufficient to keep this tyranny within comparatively narrow bounds.

Not content to demand the freedom of the Press, he required full liberty for the decent expression of opinion in every form; he was intensely eager to remove the fetters by which an unscrupulous executive, with the aid of a pliant judiciary, had sought to restrain the honest expression of opinion on matters of public interest, whether political or religious. In his eyes, such persecution was not only an act of immorality in one of the most mischievous shapes, but "a sort of confession or presumptive evidence of non-belief in the very opinions which the persecutor thus professes to support. " Writing to Richard Carlile, who lay imprisoned in Dorchester Gaol, Bentham explained: "Whatever your opinions may be, had they been opposite to what they are, my weak endeavours towards your support, under the oppression you are enduring, would not have been otherwise than they are.... Nor should I regard with less sympathy and indignation any persecution for opinions directly opposite to mine in every point than for opinions directly coincident with my own in every point." To him, as a friend of mankind, the oppressed, whosoever they might be, were the objects of sympathy; and, accordingly, on December 9th, 1824, he sent £5 to the Catholic Association " in the humble and cordial hope that his oppressed brethren of the Catholic persuasion would neither retaliate persecution by persecution, nor attempt redress by insurrection."

In fact, the great leader of the movement for Catholic Emancipation — Daniel O'Connell (1775-1847), the "Liberator of Liberators," as he styles him—was one ' Perpetual obsequious instruments in the hands of the monarch and his ministers" is Bentham's description of the judges in a letter to the *Traveller,* written in 1825. "Woe to the defendant in a political prosecution—woe to a politically obnoxious party in any suit, if the falsity of it be, though but for a moment, out of the eyes of jurors." (Bow., x. P-549-) 1790-1843; a disciple of Thomas Paine. He lay in Dorchester Gaol 1819-25.

of Bentham's intimate friends. "O'Connell," wrote the old man once, " I love you with a father's love!" The famous Irishman, in return, openly avowed himself "an humble disciple of the immortal Bentham," who constantly sought to induce in him a more tolerant spirit in religious and political controversy. Bentham, while holding himself aloof from both political parties, begged O'Connell to refrain from tirades against the Liberals, the body which comprised all to whom he could look for assistance: "Do not run amuck (Malay like) against all your friends, except a comparatively small number of zealous Catholics." Endure the conception, and even the utterance, of other men's opinions how opposite soever to your own, he would urge; and put off the advocate's gown which has but one side to it—at any rate, when you assume the mantle of the legislator.

So early as 1817 Bentham had published a collection of *Papers Relative to Codification* including certain correspondence between himself and the Emperor Alexander the First, in connection with an offer to frame a Code of Laws for Russia.

The Emperor had penned a letter of profuse thanks, sent a remembrance in the shape of a valuable ring —which was returned sealed up as it was received— and intimated that his commissioners would be commanded to ad-

dress their inquiries to Bentham, who, however, felt confident that no such inquiries would ever be made of him. This collection contained also some correspondence with James Madison, President of the United States—to whom an offer had been made Bow., iv. pp. 451-533.
of a "complete body of statute laws, or Pannomion "— and it was declared by Romilly to embrace "some of the most important views on the subject of Legislation, and on the nature of common or unwritten law, that have ever been laid before the public." Six years later there appeared the *Codification Proposal'* addressed to all nations professing Liberal opinions, accompanied by a quaint fasciculus of testimonials to the merits of the author, culled from every quarter of the globe; and, not long afterwards, Dumont published the treatise *De I'Organisation judiciaire et de la Codification.* Bentham believed that a system of laws could be so framed and expounded as to be easily understood and readily administered. By this method he hoped to get rid of the legal profession and the "demon of chicane." His ideal was undoubtedly an extravagant one; for no code can be devised so elastic as to forestall all the difficulties that may hereafter arise from the evervarying exigencies of society and commerce, nor, indeed, so complete as to embrace the solution of every problem that might result even from existing conditions. As he himself said, a single improper word in a body of laws—especially of laws given as constitutional and fundamental ones—may, perchance, prove a national calamity, and civil war may be the consequence of it. Out of one foolish word may start a thousand daggers!
His want of practical training led him, moreover, to underrate, if not to disregard, the importance of issues of fact, which cannot, in the nature of things, *Edin. Rev.,* November, 1817. Bow., iv. pp. 535-94.
be determined by reference to any code. Where ten counsel are to be found well versed in the most abstruse niceties of jurisprudence, it would not be easy to secure one thoroughly competent to grasp, marshal, and expound the inferences to be deduced from a mass of complex or conflicting oral testimony. But, however ready to detract from Bentham's merits, the critic of his work must acknowledge the debt which the whole civilised world owes to him for the impulse he gave to the provision of codes. Even in his own country it has not been without effect in certain branches of the law, and in British India his teaching has borne excellent fruit. "Had Bentham done nothing more," writes Professor Montague, "than point out the way in which the law of England could best be applied to the needs of India, he would have rendered a distinguished service to his country and to mankind."
In 1829 he published the draft of a proposed *Petition for Codification?* which he asked Burdett to present to the House of Commons. Burdett professed great devotion to him. "I hardly know," said he, " the thing you could, at least would, ask of me, that I should not feel the greatest gratification in complying with. " So far, however, as the request to present the petition was concerned, he contented himself with replying that he would "consider of it"; nor does it appear that Burdett ever undertook the task of presentation.

It has been objected to the principle of codification Notably the law relating to negotiable instruments *45 & 46 Vict, c. 61).* Edition of *Fragment on Government,* at p. 56. Bow., v. pp. 437-548.
that it requires one uniform suit of ready-made laws for all times and all states of society; but this objection rests on a misconception, for the principle relates to the *form* only of the laws, not to their *substance.* The different needs of different nations occupied Bentham's attention no less than the other manifold conditions which affect the making of laws; though it is no doubt true, as John Mill pointed out, that, taking next to no account of national character and the causes which form and maintain it, he was precluded from considering, except to a very limited extent, the laws of a country as an instrument of *national culture.* Thus he did not thoroughly appreciate that the slave needs to be trained to govern himself, the savage to submit to the government of others; but the errors into which he was led by such oversights, though fundamental in the department of constitutional law, were not, in Mill's opinion, of a nature to lead him far astray in his treatment of most branches of civil and penal legislation.
With the draft Petition for Codification was published another petition—"for Justice"—the prayer of which comprised an outline of the proposed *Judicial Establishment* and of the proposed system of *Procedure.* The volume containing these Petitions was forwarded to the Duke of Wellington in December, 1828, accompanied by a long letter begging him to become " Commanderin-Chief" of a Law Reform Association and to promote See, *eg., Influence oj Time and Place in Matters of Legislation.* (Bow., i. pp. 169-94.) *Lomlon and Westminster Review,* August, 1838.

Bentham's *Dispatch Court Bill* He was urged to put an end to the tedious formalities and ruinous delays which at that time prevailed in the Civil Courts, and to substitute therefor "the simplicity, the honesty, the straightforwardness of courts-martial!" "Your name," wrote Bentham, "will—ay, shall—be greater than Cromwell's. Already you are, as in his day he was, the hero of war. Listen to me and you will be what he tried to but could not make himself—the hero of peace—that peace which is the child of Justice." The Duke duly acknowledged the communication, and soon after received another long letter upbraiding him for his folly in engaging with Lord vvinchilsea in the famous duel on Battersea Fields. Sir H. Hardinge was, it seems, the Duke's second, while Lord Falmouth attended the Earl of Winchilsea. "On the signal being given, the Duke instantly raised his pistol and fired at his opponent, without doing him (or his clothes, as absurdly rumoured) the slightest injury. The Earl then raised his weapon and discharged it in the air." Bentham's good-humoured remonstrance brought an immediate reply from the Duke, and without any delay the old man was, in his own phrase, "at him once more." The promptness of his attention, Bentham explained, had called forth the garrulity of old age. "Wellington is very civil," he observed one day, " and gives immediate answers to letter after letter that I send him."

When O'Connell received his copy of the Petitions, Bow., iii. pp. 319-431. *John Bull* newspaper, March 29th, 1829. he at once wrote to his " revered master" for " suggestions, nay commands," as to what he should do in Parliament. "If you think it right I will begin with the Despatch Court, that is the first or second day of the Session—then the natural as opposed to technical procedure; at least, a portion on this subject—then an address to procure a *Code.* Every day I will have a petition on some one or more law abuse."

During the last fourteen years of his life, Bentham was occupied in ceaseless efforts to complete the *Constitutional Code for the Use of all Nations Professing Liberal Opinions?* The work had long been in progress; so early as 1816, indeed, extracts from the manuscripts had been printed, and an "avant courrier" in the form of *Leading Principles* was published in 1823. The first volume made its appearance in 1830, and the other two were then in such a state of forwardness that little was needed for their completion. "Were the Author to drop into his last sleep while occupied in the tracing of these lines," wrote Bentham in the Preface, " able hands are not wanting from which the task of laying the work before the public would receive its completion." But although the old man was still busy at work within three weeks of his death—" codifying like any dragon," as he put it—the book was not published in its integrity until 1841. The Code has been described as the most comprehensive, as well as the most mature, of all his works: its influence in many countries was considerable —and it has been said that, of all the great reforms Letter from Derrynane Abbey, dated October 22nd, 1829. (Bow., xi. p. 22.) Bow., voL ix. *Ibid.,* ii. pp. 267-74.

which followed his death, none was more Benthamic than those which built up the modern system of local government in England. It undoubtedly contains throughout many interesting and fruitful suggestions, but—except in the first book—it is replete with uninviting detail, and the style is often such as to repel even the most resolute reader.

A print depicting the interior of the House of Lords during the investigation known as "the Queen's Trial," displays Bentham in a rather prominent position. Oddly enough made up the group will be, he wrote to Dr. Parr: "Before and quite close to me is an old acquaintance of former years, Sir Humphrey Davy; then comes that 'servile poet and novelist,' Sir Walter Scott, and next to Scott that 'ultra-servile sack guzzler,' Southey." "I shall laugh heartily," replied Parr, "to see your figure by 'those reptiles,' Walter Scott and Southey": for it was well known that Bentham did not admire poets, and, indeed, never read poetry with enjoyment, although he would grant that doggerel might prove useful for the purpose of "lodging facts more effectually in the mind." It is, however, only fair to record that he was as sturdy an advocate of liberty of taste as of liberty of conscience, and that one of the " reptiles," at any rate, had provoked strong language by the violence of his attacks on all who maintained popular opinions. Bentham and Parr were not the only men of liberal ideas who bore a grudge Redlich and Hirst s *English Local Government,* i. pp. 90, 91.

This print was published by Bowyer on June 1st, 1823; but the position of those grouped near Bentham was altered before publication. against Southey. In 1794 he had written a piece entitled "Wat Tyler," which asserted in extravagant terms the claims of the people to equality of rights and a division of property. Some twenty-three years later, those whom he was used to assail as Jacobins caused the piece to be published, whereupon the author —then become Poet Laureate—applied for an injunction to restrain its publication. But Lord Eldon, to Southey's infinite chagrin, refused the application on the ground that, the work being " of a most dangerous tendency," its author was not entitled to claim relief.

On one occasion, we are told, "the hermit" went out to dine—a most rare adventure, says Bowring. It was at Hendon.with George Grote (1794-1871), the historian of Greece, who had been introduced to his guest by Ricardo. In 1825 he paid a brief visit to Paris, being abroad just a month. The object of this visit—*son voyage triomphal a Paris,* M. Hal£vy calls it—was to consult a physician as to the treatment of a cutaneous disorder from which he was at that time suffering; and according to a family tradition, he was attended by Thomas Hodgskin in the capacity of secretary. He saw his old friend Lafayette and was much gratified by his reception in the French capital. Once, as he entered the Courts of Justice, the whole Bar rose to welcome him, and the President insisted that the famous English jurist should occupy the seat of honour at his right hand.

In the early part of February, 1832, less than four Romilly's *Memoirs,* iii. p. 285.

Thomas Hodgskin, par Elie Halevy (1903), p. 85. months before his death, Bentham received, with sincere pleasure, a renowned statesman, whom he had not met for nearly forty years. Talleyrand had long held the genius of Bentham in high esteem. He had advocated the building of a Panopticon in Paris, and shown a lively interest in the publication of the *Trails de Legislation,* offering to charge himself with the costs of a complete edition if the publisher feared the speculation. Once when Bowring observed that from no modern writer had so much been stolen as from Bentham, and stolen without acknowledgment—Talleyrand assented, adding: *Et pilUpar tout le monde, il est toujours riche.* "Do you want an appetite, Prince?" wrote the old man: "The means of finding one for *Friday* next is to come to this retreat, and take a Hermit's dinner on *Thursday!*—" To dine with Bentham —to dine alone with Bentham," replied Talleyrand; "that is a pleasure which tempts me to break an engagement I have been under for several days."

So early as the summer of 1831 Bentham remarked that his memory was occasionally impaired; his spirits became, at times, less buoyant; and he more than once expressed the belief that these symptoms betokened a sure, if gradual, break-up of the system. Indeed, from the spring of the following year, the old man, though still able to write and capable of sustained thought, calmly awaited death, which took place on the 6th June, 1832. As the end drew near, he said to the friend watching by his side, " I now feel that I am dying; our care must be to minimise pain. Do not let the servants come into the room, and keep away the youths; it will be distressing to them, and they can be of no service." His head resting on Bowring's bosom, he became gradually colder, and the muscular powers were deprived of action: it was an imperceptible passing. "After he had ceased to speak, he smiled and grasped my hand, looked at me affectionately, and closed his eyes. There was no struggling, no suffering; life faded into death, as the twilight blends the day with darkness." With a view to the advancement of science, he directed that his body should be dissected. This injunction was obeyed, and gave Matthew Arnold occasion for much elaborated merriment at the expense of the faithful Benthamite—"On a pious pilgrimage to obtain from Mr. Bentham's executors a secret bone of his great dissected master." The skeleton, covered with the clothes he commonly wore, and supporting a waxen effigy of his head, is carefully preserved in the Anatomical Museum of University College, London. Across one knee rests his favourite stick, " Dapple," and at the foot of the figure lies the skull, with the white hairs of the old man still clinging to its surface.

"He never knew prosperity and adversity, passion nor satiety," wrote John Mill: "he never had even the experience which sickness gives; he lived from childhood to the age of eighty-five in boyish health. He knew no dejection, no heaviness of heart. He never felt life a sore and weary burthen. He was a boy to the last." Like a boy, too, he was eager for praise Montague's *Fragment on Government,* p. 14.

Essays on Criticism (First Series), Preface (1865), p. x. Mill's *Early Essays,* by Gibbs, p. 349. and ready to take affront. Apt, as he was, to embrace the passing compliments of courtesy as deliberate judgments on his merits, his complacent acceptance of such civilities lent colour to the charge of excessive vanity which, with some show of justice, has been so often levelled against him. Yet in his personal relations he was, in no sense, arrogant, boastful, or ill-mannered. "The way to be comfortable," wrote he on sending, in his eighty-fourth year, an autograph to Lady Hannah Ellice, "is to make others comfortable; the way to make others comfortable is to appear to love them; the way to appear to love them is to love them in reality. *Probatur ab experientia* per Jeremy Bentham, Queen's Square Place, Westminster. Born Feb. 15: anno 1748. Written (this copy) 24 Oct. 1831." "His moral life," said Dumont, "is as beautiful as his intellectual. " Never did any philosopher better conform his life to his doctrines. Rush tells us that at table he talked but little, and had a benevolence of bearing suited to the philanthropy of his mind. "He seemed to be thinking only of the convenience of his guests.... Bold as are his opinions in his works, here he was wholly inobtrusive of theories that might not have commanded the assent of all present." He made it a rule to avoid discussion with those whose opinions were so remote from his own as to render discussion fruitless. A moralist, like a surgeon, he once remarked, should never wound, but to heal. Say not "I have a right to proclaim and defend my opinion": What is *Edin. Rev.,* vol. xxix. p. 217. *Residence at Court of London,* p. 286.

P the English of all that? "I have a right to give pain— to make enemies—to have backs turned, and doors shut against me."

Two years after Bentham's death Francis Place referred to him as " my constant, excellent, venerable preceptor, of whom I think every day of my life, whose death I constantly lament, whose memory I revere, and whose absence I deplore "; and it is safe to affirm that more than one distinguished man, both in the Old World and the New, shared Place's sorrow, and with him mourned the loss of a venerated teacher.

Although brought up in the tenets of the Church of England, Bentham does not seem to have accepted any theological creed. While strongly opposed to the maintenance of religious establishments by the State, he in no way concerned himself with questions of dogma, until in later years he was aroused to active hostility by the attitude of the clergy on educational issues; indeed, in his elements of *Penal Law,* he suggests that the services of religion in prisons should be rendered attractive so as to become efficacious, and that the chaplain, by his kindly offices, should constitute himself a "daily benefactor—a friend to console and to enlighten." In his view, the adoption of dogma—even false dogma—might in certain circumstances promote the general happiness, and so conform to the principle of utility.

During the last fourteen years of Bentham's life there appeared several works on theological subjects written by him or based upon his notes. In 1818, *Church-of* Wallas' *Life of Place,* p. 92.

Englandism and its Catechism examined, preceded by Strictures on the Exclusionary System as pursued in the National Society's Schools; in 1822, *An Analysis of the Influence of Natural Religion, by Robert Beauchamp* (edited by Grote); in 1823, *Not Paul but Jesus by Gamaliel Smith,* a work which had been put together by Place in 1817. These productions contain some trenchant writing on the evils of clericalism, but are of no more permanent value than the theological essays of Sir Isaac Newton. In some passages the subjects are treated with much levity, and the whole of these writings are excluded from the collected edition of the works by Bowring, who did not share the Master's views on theological topics. "Jug" (short for Juggernaut), with its derivatives " juggical," "anti-jug," etc., was used by Bentham and his friends as a "conveniently unintelligible synonym" for orthodox Christianity. But, fiercely as he sometimes wrote on these subjects, he always stood out boldly for universal toleration: every man, he would say, is master of his own actions, no man of his own opinions. Written some years earlier. *Mother Church of England relieved by Bleeding* (1823) and the *Book of Church Reform* (1831) are extracted from this treatise. Wallas' *Life of Place,* p. 82. CHAPTER IX BENTHAM'S CREED AND AIMS

"A BENTHAMITE! What sort of animal is that?"—the founder of the Benthamic school inquired of M. Dumont in 1802—"I can't find such a word in Boyer's Dictionary. Utilitarian would be the more *propre* term." This word "utilitarian," which was already acquiring, as M. Haldvy puts it, *une deception pejorative,* had been applied by Bentham some twenty years before to one Joseph Townsend—"a parson, brother to the Alderman "—whom he described as "a utilitarian, a naturalist, a chemist, a physician." But despite Bentham's protest, " Benthamite" was for half a century the epithet commonly used to designate the older generation of utilitarians, a body of men who, while less speculative, and perhaps less scientific, than their immediate successors in this school of philosophy, exerted more influence upon practical legislation.

The axiom of " utility "—that the greatest happiness of the whole community ought to be the end pursued in all human actions—is one inseparably linked with *1739-1816.* Rector of Pewsey; Fellow of Clare Coll., Camb. ; author of several works; he was, said Bentham, " beloved by everybody." Mr. Wallas takes 1824 as marking the change of era; *Life of Place,* P..85.

the name of Bentham, though he made no pretension to be the discoverer of a principle which, as we have already seen, had formed a fundamental doctrine of many earlier writers. How, then, was this end—this "greatest possible happiness"—to be attained? In Bentham's view, Nature has placed mankind under the governance of two sovereign masters, *pleasure* and *pain.* He sought to measure the good or evil of an action solely by the quantity of pleasure or pain—physical or intellectual—resulting from it. The greatest happiness would flow, therefore, from a supreme blend of pleasures; and it obviously became essential for him to devise some scheme of " moral arithmetic" for the determination of the various "lots" of pleasure and pain, some sort of " felicific calculus," with elements or dimensions of value, such as would enable him to measure the good or evil of the consequences which actions tend to produce. The greatest sum of happiness would, he held, accrue to the community by each individual member of it doing the utmost to increase his own —not necessarily by the pursuit of immediate pleasure, but by doing that which, possibly at the cost of present pain, would ultimately secure him a balance of pleasure. Bentham did not, however, deal fully or even consistently with this "self-preference" principle, nor did he make clear whether it rested on anything more than assumption. He was, indeed, far from encouraging individual selfishness. No, we must not add force to a passion already sufficiently strong! "Society is held together only by the sacrifices that men can be induced to make of the gratifications they demand; to obtain these sacrifices is the great difficulty, the great task of government."

In the later years of his life Bentham came to the conclusion that the phrase " The greatest happiness of the greatest number" was wanting in clearness and precision. He accordingly substituted for this phrase the simpler expression, "The greatest happiness," as representing the true object of politics and morals. The "greatest number" he dismissed as superfluous; and thus, says Colonel Thompson, one of his most capable disciples, " the magnificent proposition emerged clearly, and disentangled from its accessory." Now, the "accessory proposition" is that the greatest aggregate of happiness must always include the happiness of the greatest number; and this assertion Colonel Thompson regards as manifestly true. He assumes, first of all, that the greatest number must always be composed of those who individually possess a comparatively small portion of the good things of life; and then he goes on to argue that, if anything is taken from one of these to give to another whose possessions are greater, it is plain that what he loses in happiness is greater than what the other gains. Half a crown is of infinitely more consequence to the porter who loses it than to the duke who may chance to find it. A chief part of the baseness of the rich man, who seized the ewe lamb of his poor neighbour, consisted in doing that which caused so much greater pain to the sufferer than happiness to the receiver 2

This reasoning may perhaps be sound on the as Bow., ii. p. 497; and see *ibid.,* ix. p. 192.

Col. Perronet Thompson's *Works,* i. p. 136.

sumption made by Colonel Thompson, if it be further assumed that happiness is synonymous with opulence, and that there is a given limited amount of wealth to be distributed arbitrarily among the various members of the community; but " the greatest happiness of the greatest number," clearly involves both the intensity of the happiness and the number of persons among whom it is diffused, and it cannot be lopped of its "greatest number" as one might eliminate the word "right" where it recurs in the phrase, "the right man in the right place." Although Bentham's aim was undoubtedly to diffuse happiness amongst the greatest possible number of persons, it is manifest that a measure which conferred happiness in a high degree upon each member of a large minority might, in certain circumstances, be preferable to one which gave a much lower degree of pleasure to each member of the numerical majority. May it not be that Bentham was moved to reject the latter clause of his famous formula by some doubt as to the truth of the "accessory proposition" rather than by the mere perception of superfluity? We are inclined to ask whether the formula, in either shape, connotes any really definite idea; certainly the involved and pseudomathematical statements extracted by Bowring from the *Deontology* contain no lucid reason for the change, nor throw any light on the difficulties that surround Bentham's interpretation of his axiom. It would seem, Bow., i. pp. 18-19. The *Deontology,* or *Science of Morality,* was published in 1834, and, as the edition was not exhausted, is not included by Bowring in the collected works. It is an unsatisfactory book, and is generally supposed to represent the views of its editor (Bowring) rather than those of Bentham. *(Sect if.* Albee's *Utilitarianism,* p. I77n.) indeed, that in order to reduce the " greatest happiness" principle to a form which embodies a definite, accurate, and intelligible proposition, we must state it as follows: If it be assumed that the *happiness* which a man derives from the enjoyment of his *property* increases with the amount of the property but at a *diminishing* rate, then a *given* amount of property divided amongst a *given* population will produce the greater aggregate amount of happiness the more nearly the division approaches equality of distribution. The truth of this proposition may be readily and rigidly demonstrated; but, as will be seen from the nature of the hypotheses, it can prove of little or no practical value.

That Bentham attached too high a degree of importance to the doctrine of utility will be generally admitted; but, in the opinion of John Mill who knew him well, we probably owe all that he did to its adoption. It was, says Mill, necessary to him to find a first principle which he could receive as self-evident, and from which he could derive all his other doctrines as logical consequences.

Armed with this principle of " utility" as with some brand Excalibur, he deemed himself fully equipped to encounter any difficulty, to remove any obstacle, that should present itself in the wide range of morals, politics, or law. It is not surprising to find that his equipment proved inadequate, more particularly in the department of morals—for neither pleasure nor pain can be expressed in terms which admit a rigid application of the rules of arithmetic and algebra.

Early Essays, by Gibbs, p. 376.

In the year 1817 he published, with explanatory notes and observations, the remarkable *Table of the Springs of Action* purporting to show the several species of pleasures and pains of which man's nature is susceptible, together with the various interests, devices, and motives respectively corresponding to them. The collation of appellatives," neutral, eulogistic and dyslogistic," affords a curious, if not very informing, ensample of Bentham's peculiar treatment of ethical questions; and although psychologists deem the table absurd, especially if taken as setting forth the elementary or "simple" feelings, it probably contained as much psychology as was required for the exposition of his legislative theories. It must, indeed, ever be borne in mind that the real end and aim of all his labours was *practical legislation*—a great part of his writings, says Sir Leslie Stephen, may be regarded as so much raw material for Acts of Parliament—and it will be allowed that in the field of law, at any rate, he met with conspicuous success. Dr. Albee goes so far as to declare that Bentham contributed almost nothing of importance to the science of ethics, or " deontology," as he himself phrased it, and further, deplores his attempt to reduce that science to "moral arithmetic" in the "grimly literal sense." But even Dr. Albee concedes that he unquestionably did more than any of his contemporaries to bring the Utilitarian theory into popular ethical discussions, and admits that his short Bow., i. pp. 195-219. First printed in 1815, but compiled, for the most part, at a much earlier period. Stephen's *Utilitarians,* i. p. 252.

comings as a philosopher may be assigned in part to the fact that his works treat primarily of jurisprudence. We should, therefore, never forget that "moral arithmetic " had not as its main object the creation of an ethical code, but rather the founding of a science of law and the establishment of a basis for the theory of legal rewards and punishments.

It has been said that there is scarce an argument in Bentham's voluminous writings which is not to the purpose so far as it goes, and it certainly would not be easy to discover many instances of false reasoning. In applying to actions the tests of " moral arithmetic," his premisses are sometimes inaccurate and often incomplete; but, if we assume the validity and sufficiency of his premisses, we must admit that his reasoning is generally sound and his conclusions just.

The defects and limitations of his doctrines, as well as his personal disqualifications for the great task which he imposed upon himself, have formed the subject of much friendly comment and more hostile criticism. His own mind viewed as a" representative of universal human nature " was, we are told, singularly incomplete. He had enjoyed but scant experience of the various and ever-varying sorts and conditions of men. He failed to sympathise with many of the strongest feelings that direct the thought and action of mankind, and he lacked the power of imagination, says Mill: he sought not only to construct philosophy out of materials furnished by his own mind, but to construct it without regard to the lessons of history, and without any reference to *History of English Utilitarianism* (1902), p. 1go.
-Stephen's *Utilitarians,* i. p. 316.
the opinions of his predecessors, whose views he dismissed as "vague generalities." Now, no man's synthesis can be more complete than his analysis, Mill continues; and it never seems to have occurred to Bentham that these same vague generalities contained the whole unanalysed experience of the human race— while the collective mind may not penetrate *below* the surface, it nevertheless sees *all* the surface.

Regarding the nations of the earth as aggregates of beings fashioned in a mould of his own creation and bent on the pursuit of their own selfish interests, unmoved either by purely generous impulses or by the violence of passion, he was led to believe that the whole duty of man might be enforced by the operation of *Sanctions;* that is to say, certain pains and pleasures so annexed to actions as to form chains, as it were, binding a man to the observance of some particular rule of life or conduct. He considered that there are four distinguishable sources from which such pleasures or pains are used to flow: *(a)* the *physical* sanction, pleasures or pains naturally arising in the course of human conduct; *ib)* the *political,* or, as it might perhaps be termed, the legal sanction, dependent on the law of the land; *(c)* the *moral,* or popular sanction, operating through the moral habits of existing society without reference to the directions of the legislator; and *(d)* the *religious* sanction, operating through some superior being. Of these four sanctions the physical is alto *Early Essays,* by Gibbs, p. 346.

Bentham afterwards treated the sanction of *sympathy* as separate from the *physical* sanction, *i.e.,* he distinguished between pleasure or pain coming to a man directly, and pleasure or pain coming, as it were, by reflexion—through the medium of pleasure or pain regarded as having place in the breast of another. (Bow., iii. p. 290.) gether the groundwork of the political and the moral, as also of the religious, in so far as it bears relation to the present life. Bentham takes as an illustration the case of a man's goods being consumed by fire. If this happen by pure accident, it is simply a calamity; if by reason of his own imprudence, it may be styled a punishment of the physical sanction; if by the sentence of the magistrate, a punishment of the political sanction; if for want of assistance withheld by his neighbour from some dislike to his *moral* character, a punishment of the moral sanction; if through distraction of mind occasioned by the dread of God's displeasure, a punishment of the religious sanction.

The real meaning which Bentham attached to the sanctions (especially to the physical sanction) may, perhaps, be best gathered from his own observations in relation to an offence characterised by cruelty. He is considering to what extent the atrocity of a supposed offence should operate in determining the force of evidence required to prove its commission. "In such a case," says he, " the seducing motives have to contend with the motive of humanity, sympathy, general benevolence (take which name you will)—to contend with it in its character of a restraining, a tutelary motive. The disposition of the individual in question being given (that is, the effective force with which it habitually acts upon his mind)—the greater the degree of cruelty said to be displayed in the offence said to be committed, the greater the force with which, on that particular occasion, the motive in question must have opposed the perpetration of it. But the principle of humanity is but one of several principles, which, on every such occasion, are acting upon the human mind in the character of tutelary and restraining principles. There are, besides this, the three respective forces of the political, the moral or popular, and the religious sanctions. Neither is this by any means the most intense and uniform in its operation, of the four tutelary forces. It may or may not be stronger than the force of the religious sanction—it may or may not be stronger than that of the moral—but it never can be accounted comparable in strength to that of the political sanction. Many men fear the wrath of Heaven; many men fear loss of character; but all men are acted upon, more or less, by the fear of the gaol, the scourge, the gallows, the pillory, and so forth. In this point of view, whatever improbability is given to the supposed offence by those other restraining motives, the additional improbability given to it by the circumstance in question seems scarce worth taking into the account. On the other hand, the force of the political and moral sanctions acts upon a man in the character of restraining motives, only upon the supposition of discovery. The force of humanity has this in common with that of the religious sanction, that the supposition of discovery is not necessary to the application of it; and, besides the comparatively greater extent of its operation when contrasted with the religious sanction, the principle of humanity (whatever may be the force with which it acts) is surer to be present to the mind."

Bentham's rigid adherence to the dogma that morality depends upon determinate consequences and not upon motives, coupled with his disregard of the more subtle moral influences, undoubtedly led him astray in the discussion of some of the nicer questions of individual behaviour and social development. But his vigorous, self-reliant, and practical mind was admirably fitted to analyse and classify the *material* interests of society —to regulate the mere business part of our social arrangements. His mistake, says Mill, simply consisted in supposing that the business part of human affairs was the whole of them. Now, as law happens to be a matter of business—is, in fact, the business part of human affairs—he was able, after many years of constant labour, to determine the nature of the "political" sanctions conducive to happiness, and to achieve a memorable triumph in the department of legislation. It has been said that before Bentham's day no one had ever dared to speak disrespectfully of English law or of the British Constitution. But the assault of this arch-innovator was as bold as it was long-sustained; countless absurdities passing current as rules of evidence, astounding fictions spreading over the whole field of jurisprudence, cunning devices for plundering suitors and enriching officials, all were ruthlessly exposed. He would have no commerce with mere abstractions. "The more abstract the proposition is," said he, "the more liable is it to involve a fallacy." He insisted on a rigorous application of the " method of detail." He would never reason about a whole until it had first been resolved into its component parts. He classified and reclassified, and would accept no formula which could not be interpreted in terms of definite facts. "Hasty generalisation," he cried, "the great stumbling-block of intellectual vanity!—hasty generalisation, the rock that even genius itself is so apt to split upon!—hasty generalisation, the bane of prudence and of science!"

In the preceding chapters we have dealt with Bentham's views on the subject of Punishment. Some indication has been given of the nature of his work in relation to Codification, the abolition of the Usury Laws, Prison Discipline, the Poor Laws, Local Government, the Administration of Oaths, Law Taxes, Savings Banks, the Laws of Real Property, the Patent Laws, etc. Many of the salutary reforms which he struggled to effect have long been accomplished; and as a result some of his most valuable writings are to-day rarely read, or even referred to, with any just appreciation of their merits. His books would now be more esteemed had his work been less effective. The two volumes on *Judicial Evidence,* for example, relate largely to anomalies and abuses which have since disappeared; yet these volumes contain many chapters of absorbing interest, full of valuable suggestion to the mind of any man concerned with the study of law.

The *Introductory View* was prepared by James Mill and partly printed in 1812; but more than one bookseller, we are told, declined to be responsible for the publication, fearing lest it should be held to constitute a libel on the administration of justice. Dumont's *Trait/* Cf. Stephen's *Utilitarians,* p. 317. Bow., vi. pp. 1-187.

des Preuves Judiciaires, published at Paris in 1823, contained, however, in a condensed form Bentham's general speculations on the subject, and an English version appeared in 1825. Two years later the lengthy treatise known as the *Rationale of Evidence* was published, in five volumes, under the editorship of John Mill, then a young man barely twenty-one years of age. It had been begun three times, at considerable intervals, each time in a different manner and each time without reference to the preceding undertaking. "One service," writes Mr. Wallas, " which all Bentham's disciples were allowed to perform, was the writing of Bentham's later books." According to Sir James Mackintosh, these disciples resembled the auditors of an Athenian philosopher, and gathered their opinions rather from the familiar conversation of the Master than from the written word; but John Mill declares that it was his father who exercised *personal* sway over the younger men, while Bentham's influence was exerted mainly through his writings.

A verbose and acrimonious review of the treatise on Evidence appeared in the *Edinburgh.* It was a personal attack upon the author and his youthful editor rather than a criticism of the work itself. The writer denounced the "slovenly and careless confidence with which the office of editor had been performed," and, turning upon Bentham, added, coarsely and churlishly enough, "a man who wilfully leaves his brats with a nursery girl can scarcely be astonished should he find that they are not washed and combed, holes darned, Bow., vi. and vii. *Life of Place,* p, 83. Hal., ii. p. 292.

and heads scrutinised, as accurately as might be desired." Bentham taxed Brougham with having "let slip the dogs of war" at him—" in the *Edinburgh,* and perhaps elsewhere"—but Brougham gave an unqualified denial to the charge, and, indeed, asserted that he had a correspondence of weeks, and all but a rupture, with Jeffrey on the subject: "How could you listen to such a tale of tales as that *I* of all your friends ever could have let slip the dogs in E. R. at you?"

Anyhow, the reviewer—doubtless a professional lawyer —was manifestly chagrined at Bentham's supposed determination, as he interpreted it, "to put a *caput lupinum* on the lawyer's shoulders, and turn him into the wilderness as the general scapegoat for the sins of society." But the author's vigorous and masterly onslaught upon the abuses and anomalies then prevalent in the Courts —marred as it undoubtedly is by divers eccentricities of style and some unnecessary violence of diction—was recognised, even by this irate lawyer, as a "great work," containing grains of mustard seed that some day would be trees.

Bentham's object was to ascertain the best method of proceeding to investigate truth by means of "evidence" or "judicial proof"—the medium through which the results of jurisprudence must needs be obtained. It was high time, declared the *Edinburgh* in a review of Dumont's treatise, that the judicial authorities, then as ever, ready to mistake their own decisions for the voice of reason, should be undeceived; that the stagnant *Edin. Rev.,* vol. xlviii. p. 457.

November 19th, 1830; Bow., xi. p. 61. Vol. *xL* p. 170. Q atmosphere of the Courts, thronged by eager and obsequious crowds, should be stirred and purified by the fresh air of common-sense. *Vos de reo, de vobis populus Romanus judicabit.*

Legal matters, we are told, were at this time among the most fashionable topics of conversation. The cause of law reform had just lost a resolute and fearless champion by the deplorable death of Romilly—the gentle and enlightened lawyer who avowed that " every day he disliked the profession of the law the more, the more he met with success in it." Branded as a Jacobin, a hypocritical pretender to humanity, a wanton destroyer of those establishments which form the safeguards of society, he had borne "for the testimony of truth," with a serene equanimity amounting almost to indifference, constant obloquy and "reproach far worse to bear than violence."

There was assuredly sore need of activity on the part of law reformers. In the civil courts, the rule which excluded the evidence of persons interested in the result of the litigation forbade the very parties to the suit from bearing oral testimony to the facts within their knowledge. Plaintiffs and defendants were alike condemned to sit silent spectators of the trial and ofttimes to witness some grievous miscarriage of justice which might have been readily averted had they been suffered to testify. Bentham urged the abolition of this and many another barbarous rule of law. He announced, at the outset of his work, as one Cf., *e.g.,* the case of *Bardell* v. *Pickwick,* the issue of which might have been different had Mr. Pickwick been allowed to give evidence.

of his three main propositions, that an objection, the effect of which is to exclude the testimony of a witness altogether, ought not to be allowed—that is, ought not to be allowed under some pretence that the exclusion would tend to rectitude of decision. His rule was, Let in the light of evidence; and he would grant only one exception — where the letting in of such light would be attended with preponderant collateral inconvenience, in the shape of vexation, expense, or delay; for even evidence, said he, even justice itself, like gold, may be bought too dear. He accordingly maintained that the evidence of interested persons should be received, and that it should be left to the jury to make allowance for all such circumstances as might reasonably be supposed to affect the credibility of the deponent.

The other two main propositions of his treatise were in the nature of problems which he proposed to solve. What means can be adopted to secure the truth of evidence? and, What rules can be laid down for estimating the probability of the truth of evidence? His solutions of these two problems constitute a masterpiece of cogent argument and exhaustive exposition.

So far as the procedure of the *criminal* courts was concerned, he proved to be a less drastic reformer. In ordinary cases of felony, involving penalties of death or exile, the counsel for the prisoner was not, until the year 1836, permitted to address the jury on any of the facts charged against his client. It was argued that the judge was, in truth, counsel for the prisoner— the most trite and the most absurd of all false and foolish dicta, said Sydney Smith. In April, 1824, George Lamb presented to Parliament a petition from jurors at the Old Bailey, praying that counsel should be allowed to prisoners accused of felony; but such was Bentham's prejudice against professional lawyers —" hirelings of the law, purchasable male prostitutes," he called them—that he had little or nothing to urge against this rule of practice. He merely remarked that the founders of English jurisprudence were so jealous of the power of rhetoric over the affections of the jury, that, by putting a gag into the advocate's mouth, they determined to give to the jury the same sort of security that Ulysses, when among the Syrens, gave to his companions—by putting wax into their ears.

Bentham was, moreover, so apprehensive of the dangers resulting from an improper acquittal that he was inclined to approve the French method of interrogating prisoners—at any rate, he preferred it to the then existing English practice based on the maxim, *nemo tenetur se ipsum accusare.* Had he enjoyed a larger experience at the Bar, he would, we think, have been more impressed by the dangers that must ever attend the compulsory examination of accused persons. He would have been more alive to the supreme necessity of securing—even when such testimony is given voluntarily—a competent judge, who would not fail to remind the jury that the stoutest hearts may be subdued by confinement and anxiety, that it is easy to mistake righteous indignation for truculence, or *1784-1834.* Brother of second Lord Melbourne; afterwards UnderSecretary of State in the Home Department.

confound misery with remorse, and to warn them, too, that innocent men may well be led into the suppression or falsification of facts, an accepted badge of guilt. Romilly narrates a case which came under his notice, in 1807, as Solicitor-General, where an absolutely innocent young man, charged with mutiny on the *Hermione* in 1797, thinking to excite the compassion of his judges, in effect admitted his guilt, but pleaded extreme youth and his dread of the mutineers. He was sentenced to death and executed, although his relatives had procured from the Navy Office a certificate showing that at the time of the mutiny he was serving as a boy on board the *Marlborough,* far from the scene of the offence alleged against him.

It would seem, indeed, that Bentham failed to realise the extent to which the sense of security and men's confidence in the awards of the law may be impaired by the fact of a wrongful conviction; and it has been suggested that, in this particular, he was a follower of Archdeacon Paley, who opined that a prisoner, led to the block to suffer for a crime of which he is wholly innocent, ought to solace himself with the reflection that "he who falls by a mistaken sentence may be considered as falling for his country!" If this indeed be so, it is consoling to find that the eminent divine was followed by the philosopher with somewhat reluctant feet and at a respectful distance. (Cf. *ante,* p. 140.)

It was, in truth, not on advocacy, nor on rigorous rules of evidence, but on *publicity,* that Bentham mainly relied as the safeguard of testimony. He called pub *Moral and Political Philosophy* (4th edition), vol. ii. p. 302.

licity the "soul of justice"; for, while only a few individuals are gainers by *real* justice, to make its usefulness general it must *appear* as well as exist. "The most tyrannical magistrate," he declared, "becomes moderate, the most daring circumspect, when, exposed to the view of all, he feels that he cannot pronounce a judgment without being judged himself. "

Amidst his many other valuable contributions to systematic jurisprudence it is difficult to make choice, but we may well recall, as of special service to the State, Bentham's exposure of the laws relating to Bankruptcy, Insolvency, and Imprisonment for Debt. He showed with minute elaboration how the property of debtors, instead of being applied to the " undignified purpose" of satisfying their debts, was transferred to "the dignified function of contributing to the fund provided for the remuneration of legal science."

The wretched piece of legislative patchwork which has bankruptcy for its subject—to adopt his own designation—was at once complex, crude, and illadministered. The great bankers and merchants of the City of London complained that assignees plundered the debtor's estate and misapplied his assets, while the penal clauses, though of the utmost rigour were wholly ineffective. A bankrupt was required, on pain of death, to appear to his commission and make full discovery of his estate. Unless his difficulties clearly arose from some casual loss, he might, after being set in the pillory for two hours, have one of his ears nailed thereto and cut off. Convictions, how Cf. *Edin. Rev.* , vol. xL at p. 195.

ever, rarely took place; for men chose rather to submit patiently to the gross frauds practised upon them, says Romilly, than to become parties to the execution of such cruel and sanguinary laws.

The enactments relating to Insolvent Debtors (that is, insolvent persons who were not *traders)* stood equally in need of amendment. The distinction between Insolvency and Bankruptcy was, as Bentham clearly showed, a source of fraud and vexation to the suitor, a goldmine to the man of law. "Precious distinction! a wall of paper to fraud, a wall of adamant to justice." Speaking generally, a creditor might cast the insolvent into gaol and keep him there for life, even if he were willing to give up everything he had in the world for the satisfaction of his debts. At uncertain intervals, Parliament was driven to relieve the overflowing prisons. The general law was, for the time being, abrogated, contracts were cancelled, and the gaolers turned loose upon the world a crowd of debtors who—howsoever honest when they entered prison—had, for the most part, learned the maxims and acquired the habits of that abode of shame and misery.

Bentham did not advocate the complete abolition of imprisonment for debt. Humanity in her soft colours, said he, decks the breastplate of the debtor's Exorbitant fees were, moreover, demanded on behalf of judges, attorneys, and gaolers. At Dover Castle the fees on first commitment of a prisoner from Margate amounted to *£4 igs. rod.,* and the man might lie there, at the suit of the Crown, from ten to twenty months without trial or hearing before a court of justice. Only a very small portion of the damp, dark, and filthy courtyard was paved; the rooms were without grates, and neither mops, pails, brooms, fire, nor candles were allowed. (Neild on *Prisons,* 1812; *Edin. Rev.,* vol. xxii. p. 387.)

champion: Justice, in her grave and sombre tints, that of the champion of the injured creditors. "Ah! let him out! let him out!" cries the noble sentimentalist, who gets nothing by his being kept in. "Yes, true enough; if there he be, and have nothing wherewith to pay, nor have done anything for which it is fit he should be punished, the sooner he be let out the better. But do you know whether he have wherewith to pay? do you know how and why he came there?" These questions, said Bentham, demand careful consideration. Arrest on mesne process was, however, unreservedly condemned by him, and he probably deserves the credit of its ultimate abolition' Under this process, at the pleasure of any man, another might be arrested for an alleged debt of *£20* or more— until 1826, £10—and forthwith consigned to gaol without having any opportunity of being heard, and with no alternative than that of removal to a spunging house, should he be in a position to pay for such accommodation. The "demon of chicane," in the shape of an angel of beneficence, had, indeed, suggested "a wretched palliative," to wit, an affidavit preceding the warrant of arrest; but this affidavit contained no assurance of the creditor's belief in the necessity for the arrest, nor did it even aver that the alleged debt exceeded in amount any counterclaim or debt due *per contra.* The true course, urged Bentham, is an immediate scrutiny into the circumstances of each individual case. Firstly, to ascertain the cause of the alleged debtor's resistance to the claim, and, secondly, Bow., vi. p. 181.

to inquire as to his solvency and means of payment. But let the debtor be *punished* only when it has been shown that *blame* attaches to him. "To all such distinctions," said Bentham, "under the guidance of Judge and Co., existing Law inexorably shuts her eyes. Why? Because to make the distinctions it would be necessary for the judge to hear evidence—to hear evidence from the best source, in the best shape, and at the properest time: against all which he sits resolved." The measure of punishment would, he suggests, have been incomplete if the shorn creditor had not come in for a share of it. "While the debtor, instead of being compelled to give up what he has in his power, if anything, for the satisfaction of his creditor, is either rioting or starving in gaol—who knows or who cares which?—the injured creditor is fined 4. per day for keeping him there; and he must submit to this additional loss, or forego whatsoever chance there may be of recovering any part of his original loss."

To the student of politics Bentham's speculations are of considerable interest, though the most cursory reader may see that his examination of political problems is, generally, less exhaustive than his treatment of legal topics. We have already referred to his writings on such subjects as Free Trade, Colonial Expansion, and Parliamentary Reform. In dealing with the question of Constitutional Government, he confines himself, for the most part, to a consideration of the means best adapted to check abuses of power. The individual, he said, ought to be left to provide for his own Bow., vi. pp. 182, 183.

enjoyments; the principal function of *government* being to protect him from sufferings. This office it fulfils by creating rights which it confers upon individuals—rights with their corresponding obligations; rights of personal security, and of protection for honour; rights of property; rights of assistance in case of need.

He rested his investigations on the assumption that a people should be controlled by a numerical majority among themselves; that, in fact, it is the proper condition of man, in a well-governed state, to be under the sway of Public Opinion. He justified his assumption in this way: to afford security against misrule, the controlling authority must consist of persons whose interests accord with the end in view; that is, the attainment of good government. In other words, there must be *identity of interest* between the controlling authority—the trustees—and the community for whom the power of control is held in trust. Where, then, is this identity of interest to be found? Only, says Bentham, in the numerical majority of the people. He perceived, of course, that the majority, if it were to be thus recognised as the paramount power in society, must, in the case of large communities, ex-

ercise rule by an artificial arrangement of Representative Government. He contended that, among modern European nations, although public opinion might impose some partial check on abuses, the rulers were really guided by sinister influences, especially by what he called "interest-begotten prejudice," the inherent tendency of men—probably quite unconsciously—to make Mill's *Early Essays,* by Gibbs, p. 373.
a virtue of following their own self-interest. The only species of government which has, or can have, in view the greatest happiness of the greatest number is, he accordingly declares, a democracy; and if the community be large, there must be some arrangement for representative government. "A democracy, then, has for its characteristic object and effect the securing its members against oppression and depredation at the hands of those functionaries which it employs for its defence, against oppression and depredation at the hands of foreign adversaries, and against such internal adversaries as are not functionaries." He carefully examined the risks of abuse of power by the governing functionaries, which can only be minimised, he says, by a system of direct personal responsibility to the numerical majority. He was astute to perceive how the wishes of this majority might be defeated, alert to provide the necessary safeguards, and eager to devise means for rescuing the members of the community from oppression, and for enabling them to obtain the redress of grievances. But he failed, as John Mill points out, to recognise the necessity for maintaining, as a corrective to partial views, some standing opposition to the will of the majority. No country, says Mill, long continues progressive without some such organised opposition to the ruling power—plebeians to patricians, clergy to kings, freethinkers to clergy, kings to barons, commons to king and aristocracy. Now Bentham, he maintains, exhausted all the resources of his vast ingenuity "in riveting the yoke of public opinion closer Bow., ix. p. 47. and closer round the necks of all public functionaries," and in excluding the possibility of any exercise of influence by a minority or by the functionary's own notion of right. He had been better employed in pointing out the means by which "institutions fundamentally democratic" might best be adapted to the preservation and strengthening of individual rights, and of "reverence for the superiority of cultivated intelligence."

It is now more than threescore years and ten since Bentham died, and yet it is not easy to assign his place among the illustrious benefactors of mankind, nor even to determine his rank among English men of letters. During lifetime his fame spread throughout the civilised world, though, as we have already seen, he was left almost "a stranger in his father's house." His name, wrote Hazlitt, is little known in England, better in Europe, best of all in the plains of Chili and the mines of Mexico; but, though neglected by a great part of his countrymen, declared Rowland Hill in 1822, he is held in the highest esteem by the enlightened and honest. "A great man has gone from among us, full of years, of good works and of deserved honours. In some of the highest departments in which the human intellect can exert itself, he has not left his equal or his second behind him." Such was the verdict of the critical *Edinburgh,* perhaps the most influential periodical of his time: "He has had blind flatterers and blind detractors, flatterers who could see nothing but perfection in his style, detractors who could see nothing *Spirit of tie Age* (1824), p. I.
Life of R. Hill, by G. B. Hill; *(Journal,* August 4th, 1822.) but nonsense in his matter. He will now have judges. Posterity will pronounce its calm and impartial decision; and that decision will, we firmly believe, place in the same rank with Galileo and with Locke the man who found Jurisprudence a gibberish and left it a science."

There is, even to this day, no great writer of our language, bearing a name so familiar as that of Jeremy Bentham, whose aims and achievements are more variously esteemed. Admirers of his genius claim that scarce a possible subject of discussion can arise which may not be illumined by words of wisdom enshrined, here or there, among his many writings: others, again, who dislike his manner and have little relish for his matter, insist that he told

"a tale of little meaning though the words are strong."

Critics of every school will, however, recognise the vastness of his labours and his singleness of purpose. Whether his standard of morals, his rules of conduct, his principles in politics be approved or condemned, we hope that readers of the foregoing pages will, at least, account him one who loved his fellowmen—as rich a guerdon, perhaps, as man need desire or deserve.
Edin. Rev., vol. lv. p. 552, in a review of Dumont's *Souvenirs sur Mirabeau.* INDEX

Abbot, Charles (Lord Colchester), *21, 117,* 136
— Hints on Census Bill addressed to, 136
— Chairman of Committee on Panopticon scheme, 117
Accused persons, evidence of, 228
Advocate. See *Counsel*
Albee's, Dr., *History of Utilitarianism,* cited, 30, 215, 217
Alexander I., Emperor of Russia, correspondence with, on codification, 199
America, United States of, reference to Government of, 99, 196
Correspondence with Madison, President of, 199
American Revolution, Bentham's views as to, 23, 34
Anarchical Fallacies, publication of, no
Ancestors, fallacies as to wisdom of, 185-6
Animals, Bentham's humanity to, 8, 90, 146
— Cruelty to, should be made a crime, 145
Annual Parliaments, 162
Annuity notes, plan as to, 137
Anti-Machiavel, letters of, 89
Aristocracy, government by, 37, 234
Articles, the Thirty-nine, Bentham's subscription at Oxford, 174
Ashburton, Lord. See *Dunning*
Ashburton, Lady (Mrs. Dunning),

56. 57
Ashhurst, Sir William: his charge to Grand Jury, 127
Assigners in Bankruptcy, frauds by, 230
Auckland, Lord. See *Eden, William*
Bailey, Mr. Justice, 39.
Ballot, voting by, advocated by Bentham, 162, 176
— denounced in *Edinburgh Review,* 162
Banks, Savings or Frugality, plan for, 135
Bankruptcy, defects in law of, 230
Bankrupts, secretary of, emoluments of, 193
Bankruptcy Court Bill, criticism of Brougham's, 184
Baring, Sir Francis, 57, 137
Barr£, Colonel, 65-68, 113
Barrow Green, Bentham's residence at, 153
Beccaria: his *Crimes and Punishments,* 36, 79, 140
— comparison of, with Bentham, 144
Beccaria: *quare* whether he suggested "greatest happiness" to Bentham, 30, 36
Beckford, author of *Vathek,* reference to, 51
Bentham, Alicia, mother of Jeremy, 1. 2. 5
Bentham, George, nephew of Jeremy, 3
Bentham, Jeremiah, father of Jeremy, I, 22, 24, 26, 38, 41, 73, 89, 120
Bentham, Jeremy. See Table of Contents
Bentham, Sir Samuel, brother of Jeremy, 2, 75, 79, 1oo, 112, 117, 118
Bentham, Dr., of Christ Church, Oxford, 13, 14, 20
Bickersteth, Henry (Lord Langdale), 175
Bingham edits *Book of Fallacies,* 185
Blackstone, Sir William, Bentham's attack on *Commentaries* of, 17,23, 35
— friendship with Lord Shelburne, 43
— his Hard Labour Bill, 37, 38, 70, 72
— feud with Mansfield, 60
Blaquiere, Lieut., 189
Borrow's *Bible in Spain,* cited, 150
Bowood, Bentham's visits to, 45, 122, 125
Bowring, Sir John, biographer of Bentham, 3, 46, 189, 190
Brissot, Bentham's acquaintance with, 25, 86, 100, 108
Bristol, Lord, a visitor at Bowood, 51
Brougham, Henry (Lord), friendship with Bentham, 149,159,182, 188, 225
Brougham, Bentham's attacks on, 184
—opposes Burdett's Reform motion, 177
Browning Hill, Bentham's attachment to, 7
Burdett, Sir Francis, his friendship with Bentham, 160, 188
election for Westminster, 156, 178
— — motion for Parliamentary Reform, 176
Burke, Edmund, 86, 192
Burton, Hill, editorof *Benlhamiana,* 21. 43. 135
Buxton visited by Bentham, 18
Camden, Charles Pratt, Earl of, 41, 53. 54. *62, 63*
Capital, trade and production limited by, 107
Capital Punishment opposed by Bentham, 144
Carew, Sir Reginald Pole-, 117
Carlile, Richard, letter to, from Bentham, 198
Caroline, Queen, picture of her "trial," 205
Cartwright, Major, 161
Cats, Bentham's fondness for, 91
Catechism of Parliamentary Rejorm, 160
Catherine II. of Russia, 76
Catholics, Roman, Bentham advocates emancipation of, 198
Census, suggestions as to taking the, 136
Certainty of punishment, necessity for, 145
Chancery, delays in Court of, 128,193
Chambre, Mr. Justice, 39
Chaplains, Bentham's view as to Prison, 210
Chatham, Earl of, 45
— Second Earl of, 52
Chemistry, Bentham's fondness for study of, 31, 74
Chrestomaihia, Bentham's book on Education, 172
Christianity, Bentham's views as to, 210
Church of England, Bentham's writings on the, 211
Citizen, Bentham made a French, 100
Civil Code, Bentham's work upon, 138
Clarke, Chamberlain, a friend of Bentham, 19, 22, 169
Cobbett, William, 136, 157, 161
Cochrane, Lord, member for Westminster, 159
Cock-fighting, cruelty of, 146
Codification, Bentham's advocacy of, 76, 199
Codification Proposal, 200
Colonies, Bentham's views as to the acquisition of, 106, 171
Colquhoun, Patrick, a friend of Bentham, 136
Competency of witnesses, 226
Confusion, fallacies of, 185
Constantinople, Bentham's visit to, 78
Constitution, the British, Bentham's views as to, 36, 104, 196
Constitutional Code, publication of, 204
Coronation Oath, George III.'s excuse as to, 174
Counsel in criminal cases, 227
Courts-martial, reference to, by Bentham, 203
Cow, three acres and a, 134
Crichoff, Bentham's stay at, 78, 88
Crime, vagueness of word, 145
R
Davy, Sir Humphrey, 205
Debates in Legislative Assemblies, 97
Debt, imprisonment for, 231
Debtors, treatment of, 233
Declaration of Rights, Bentham's attack upon the, 108, 109, 11t
Defences of Economy against Burke and Rose, 192

Defence of Usury, 82
Defendant formerly not allowed to testify, 226
Democracy, government by, 234
Denman, Lord, 188
Deodands, paper on, by Bentham, 66
Deontology, 215
Deputy, payment to, indicative of proper salary for an office, *$2*
Derry, Bishop of. See *Bristol*
Dispatch Court Bill, 203
Dividends on stock, plan for receiving, 137
Dogmas, religious, uses of, 210
Draught of a Code for Organisation of Judicial Establishment, 99, 102
Duel, Wellington's, 203
— Burdett's, 156
Dumont, Bentham's relations with, 74. 9»93. 94. 9. 98, "4. «7. 137. 149
Dundas, Henry, Lord Melville, to8
Dunning, John, Lord Ashburton, 42, 54, 64, 88
Duty, interest should be united with, 85, 135, 176, 234
Economy, Political, Bentham's writings on, 170
Eden, Sir F. M., 148
Eden, William, Lord Auckland, 37. 70
Edgeworth, Lovell, 187
Education, the Chrestomathic System of, 173
Egypt, occupation of, 108
Eldon, Lord, 192-194
Indications respecting, 192
Elections, Bentham's proposals as to, 162
Electoral districts, 162
Elements of Art of Packing Special Juries, 157
Ellenborough, Lord, 157, 158
Ellice, Lady Hannah, 209
Emancipate your Colonies, 106
Equality, Bentham's views as to, 105
Equity Courts, delays and abuses of, 128, 193
Escheat vice *Taxation,* 131
Established Religion, Bentham opposed to, 210
Evidence, The Rationale of, 224
Evidence of defendant, 226
— of accused persons, 228
— exclusion of, 227
Exchequer Bills, 137
Expectation, disappointment of, 131
Fact, issues of, Code cannot dispose of, 200
Fallacies, Book of, 185
Fallacies, Anarchical, 109
Fees, exaction of exorbitant or illegal, 193, 231
Felicific calculus, 213
Fishing, Bentham's objection to, 8
Fitzherbert. See *St. Helen's*
Fitzmaurice, Lord (Earl of Wycombe). See *Wycombe.*
Fitzmaurice, Lord Edmond, *Life of Shelbume* by, cited *passim.* And see *Shelbume*
Ford Abbey, Bentham's residence at, 163, 180
Fordyce, Dr., Bentham attends lectures of, 31, 37
Forgery, prevention of, 136
Fox, Charles James, 147
Fox, Hon. Caroline, Bentham's attachment to, 49, 50, 77, 117, 119, 123, 151, 158
Fragment on Government, 35-37, 40, 69, 72, 73
France, era of Revolution in, 95
— Bentham made a citizen of, 100
Free Trade, Bentham's advocacy of, I71i I9S
French language, Bentham's knowledge of, 11
writings in the, 79, 92
Frigidarium, plan of a, 136
Frugality Banks suggested by Bentham, 135
Gabbett, Anne, wife of Romilly, 148
George II., ode on death of, 16, 89
George III. said to have replied to Anti-Machiavel, 89
— resistance to Catholic emancipation, 156, 174
— hostility to Panopticon project, 86,90
— religious attitude of, 101
Gibbs, J. W. M., J. S. Mill's *Early Essays,* edited by, cited *passim*
Gibbs, Vicary, 158
Government, Bentham's theory of, 232-236. See *Fragment* on
Graham, Sir James, letter from, 194
Grammar, Fragments on Universal, 173
Greek Committee, 189
Grenville, Lord, 152, 156
Gfreville, Lady E., 118
Grote, George, 206, 211
Grove, Alicia, mother ofBentham, 2
Halevy, E., his *La Formation du Radicalism: philosophise,* cited *passim*
Happiness, principle of Greatest, 20, 29, 30, 31, 36, 212-216
Hard Labour Bill, View ojthe, 37,71
Harris, Sir James (Earl of Malmesbury), 88
Hastings, Warren, Lord Lansdowne's support of, 75
Helv&ius, Bentham's acquaintance with works of, 10, 36, 78
Hendon, Bentham's residence near, 88, 112
Hill, Rowland, opinion of Bentham, 236
Hobgoblin Argument, fallacy of, 185
Hobhouse, J. C. (Lord Broughton), 185
Hodgskin, Thomas, 162, 166, 206
Hogarth, 147
Holland, Lord, 45, 47, 147, 160
Horner, Francis, 103
House of Lords. See *Peers*
Howard, John, 38, 84
Hulks, punishment of the, 39
Hume, David, principle of utility taken by Bentham from, 30
Hume, Joseph, noticed, 167, 188
Humphreys, real property code of, 191
Imports, restrictions on, 171, 195
Imprisonment for debt, 230
India, influence of Bentham on Code for, 201
— Mill'sHistoryof British, 153, 155, 16
Indications respecting Lord Eldon, 192
Innocent persons, conviction of, 229
Innovation, Bentham's love of, 23
Insane, exercise of franchise by the, 177
Insolvency and Bankruptcy, 230
Insolvent Debtors, Acts for relief of, 231
Interest-begotten-prejudice, 234
Interest should be united to duty, 8S. 135. '76. 234

International, word coined by Bentham, 27
International Law, 88
Intolerance, Bentham's dislike of, 205, 211
Introduction to the Principles of Morals and Legislation, 53, 94
Inventors, encouragement of,81,172
Irenaeus, letters to *Gazetteer* under name of, 26
Jacobins, Bentham's attitude towards the, 105, 108
Jeffrey, Lord, 16, 149, 152
Johnson, Dr. Samuel, 16, 42
Judges, election of, 102
— removal of, *it.*
Judicial Establishment in France, 99
Judicial Oaths, 174
Juries, the packing of Special, 157
Justice and Codification Petitions, 202
La Combe, Bentham's French tutor, II
Lafayette, 206
Lamb, George, 228
Lancasterian system of Education, 173
Language, Essay on, 173
Lansdowne, Marquis of. See *Shelburnt*
Lansdowne, Henry Marquis of, 47, "S» 152
Law, Bentham's dislike of profession of, 22, 24, 25
Law Reform, Bentham's work on, 29, 30, 102, 223
Law Taxes, 129
Leading Principles of the Constitutional Code, 204
Lecky, references to Bentham by, 83, 144
Leeds, Duke of, 15
Legislation, science of, 152
Legislative Assemblies, Essay on Tactics of, 97
Liancourt, Duke of, 92
Libel, writings on Law of, 157
Liberty, Bentham's view of, 106,197
Liberty of the Press, 157, 197
Lincoln's Inn, 17, 24
Lind, John, a friend of Bentham, 32, 33
Loans, restrictions on, 80
Local Courts, suggestion of, 102
Logic, Essay on, 173
Long, Charles (Secretary of Treasury), 130
Lords, House of. See *Peers*
Loughborough. See *Wcdderburn*
Lytton, Bulwer, cited 157
Macaulay, Lord, references to Bentham's works by, 93, no
Mackintosh, Sir James, 160, 188
Mackreth, Sir Robert, 18, 19
Madison, James, President of United States, 199
Mansfield (William Murray, Earl of), 18, 26, 34, 41, 60-62
Manual of Political Economy, 172
Markets, free, 171
Markham, Dr. (Archbishopof York), 10, 12
Martin, portrait of Lord Mansfield by, 61
Maseres, Baron, 44
Masters in Chancery, fictitious attendances of, 128, 193
Matlock, Bentham's visit to, 18
Melville. See *Dundas*
Mesne process, arrest on, 23a
Method, John Mill's commendation of Bentham's, 31
Mill, James, 29, 149, 153, 157, 162, 165-169, 185, 188, 191, 223
Mill, John Stuart, 30, 31, 82, 165, 168, 218, 222, 235
Milton, house of, in Bentham's garden, 121
Mirabeau, 47, 96, 98
Mitford, schoolfellow of Bentham, 13
Mitford, William, the historian, 8
Mitford. See *Redesdale*
Modvinoff, Admiral, 150
Monarchy. See *Fragment on Government*
Money, Aristotle on barrenness of, 83
Monopolies, colonial, 107
Montague, F. C, edition of *Fragment on Government* by, cited, 20, 106, 144, 201, 208
Montesquieu, 36, 37, 140
Moral Arithmetic, 144, 213
Morals and Legislation, Introduction to the Principles of, 94
Morellet, the Abb£, 79, 97, 98
Music, Bentham's fondness for, 10, 49, 165
Natural rights, mischief of the expression, 109
Nemo tenetur se ipsum accusare, 228
Nepean, Sir Evan, 68
New Lanark, Bentham's interest in establishment at, 163
North, Lord, 33
North, Brownlow, 33
Note Annuities, project as to, 137
Oaths, Bentham's views as to, 173
Observations on Mr. Secretary Peel's Speech, 192
Observations on Pitts Poor Law Bill, 134
O'Connell, Daniel, 198, 203
Official Aptitude Maximised, 192
Ontology, Fragment on, 173
Oxford University (Queen's College), 13. . «9.
Pains, measurement of, 213
Paley, Archdeacon, 87, 229
Pannomion, 200
Panopticon, scheme for Penitentiary, 84-87, 118, 124, 126
Paper money, monopoly of, 137
Paris, Bentham's visits to, 18, 61, 206
Parliament, Bentham's desire to enter, 113-116
Parliamentary Reform, 160, 175
Parr, Dr. Samuel, 86, 147, 205
Passive obedience, 35
Patents for inventions, 172
Pauper management, 135
Peace, Bentham an advocate of, 100
Pecuniary interest as a motive, 135
Peel, Sir Robert, 183, 184, 192
Peers, Chambers of, and Senates, 196
— trial of, by their own body, 103
Pembroke, Earl of, 51
Penal Code, 138
Penal law, limits of, 141
Penitentiary system, 38, 84
Perjury. See *Oath*
Persecution, religious, 198, 211
Petitions, Justice and Codification, 201, 202
Petty, Lord Henry. See *Lansdowne*
Physical sanction, 219
Pitt, William, the younger, 47, 52, 75. 80
Place, Francis, notices of, 29, 162, 165, 185, 210
Pleading, system of, 152
Pleasure, measurements of, 213
Poetry, Bentham's distaste for, 205
Poland, Letters on State of, 33

Police magistrates, Bill as to salaries of, 19
Political Economy. See *Economy*
Politics, Bentham's, 23, 102, 104, 196
Poniatowski, Stanislaus, 33
Poor Laws, 132
Popular (or moral) sanction, 219
Pratt. See *Camden*
Pratt, Lady Elizabeth, 50, 55, 56,63
Prejudice, interest-begotten, 234
Press, liberty of the, 157, 197
Priestley, Dr., 20, 30, 47, 101
Prisons, views as to, 38, 84
Prohibitory Commercial Systems, 195
Promissory Oaths, 173
Property, rights of, 105, 109, 197
Property, laws as to, 132, 191, 196
Protest against Law Taxes, 128
Public Opinion, influence of, 234
Publicity, importance of, in legal procedure, 229
Punishment, principles of, 140-145
Queen's Square Place, Westminster, Bentham's residence in, 120, 156, 180
Radicalism not Dangerous, 195
Radical Reform Bill, 195
Rapin's *History of England,* 9
Rationale of Evidence, 224
Rationale of Reward, 79, 172
Real Property, law as to, 191, 196
Redesdale, Lord (J. F. Mitford), 194
Redlich and Hirst's *English Local Government,* cited *passim*
Reform. See *Law, Parliamentary*
Register, General, of Real Property, 191
Religion, Bentham's, 210
Religious establishments, 210
Religious sanction, 219
Republic, Bentham's opinion as to, 1o1, 108, 196, 234
Resistance to Government, 36
Responsibility, 235
Restrictive punishments, 142
Restrictive Commercial Systems, 195
Retaliation, 195
Revenge, a barbarous motive for punishment, 140
Revolution, French, Bentham's attitude towards the, 104
Reward, Rationale of, 79, 172
Ricardo, David, 169, 188
Rich, the property of the, 197
Richmond, Duke of, 187
Rights, Declaration of, 108
Rochefoucauld, Due de la, 98, 100, 122
Romilly, Sir Samuel, 32, 90, 96, 97, 124, 127, 137, 139, 148, 152, 158, 164, 178, 193, 226, 229
Rose, Sir George, 130, 137, 192
Rosslyn-See *Wcddcrburn*
Rotten Boroughs, proposed Defence of, by Bentham, 109
Ruggles, Poor Law projects of Mr., 134
Rush, residence in court of London by, cited 180, 209
Russia, Bentham's visit to, 75-88
— reception of Bentham's writings in, 149
Sablonkofif, General, 149
Sanctions, operation of the, 143, 219
Schools, Chrestomathic, 173
Scotch Law Reform, 151
Scriveners' Company, 1
Second Chamber, 196
Secrecy of suffrage, necessity for the, 162, 176
Security, main object of civil law, 105
Self-preference principle, 213
Sentences, severity of, in Bentham's time, 145, 231
Session, Court of, reforms in practice of, 132
Shelburne, Lord (first Marquis of Lansdowne), 43,4553.74.75.77. 89, 100, 121, 122, 147, 151
Shelburne, Lady, 45-49,95,96,100, "3
Smith, Adam, remarks on Usury, 80-82
views on political economy, 170
Smith, Richard, editor of several works of Bentham, 172
Smith, the Rev. Sydney, 186, 227
Smyrna, visited by Bentham, 77
Snail's pace argument, fallacy of, 185
Somerset, Duke of, and George II., 114
Southey, Robert, 205
Spain, Bentham's interest in the affairs of, 190
Special Juries. See *Juries*
Speranski, noticed, 170
Springs of Action, Table of the, 217
St. Helens, Lord, 100, III
St Leonards, Lord, 160
Stael, Madame de, 187
Stanislaus, King of Poland, 33
Stephen, Sir Leslie, *Utilitarians,* cited *passim*
Stephen, Mr. Justice, *reference to Bentham by,* 155
Stewart, Dugald, reference to Bentham by, 83
Style, variations in Bentham's, 27-29
Subdivisions, Bentham's minute, 94, 222
Succession, taxes on, 131
Suffrage, Bentham's approval of universal, 162, 176
Supply without Burden, 131
Swear not at all, 173
Sydney, Lord, 187
Sympathy as a sanction, 219
Tactics, Political, Essay on, 97
Talleyrand, his appreciation of Bentham, 207
Taxes on justice denounced, 129
Telemachus, influence of, in Bentham, II
Testimony, improper rejection of, 226
Thompson, W., of Cork, letter to, 182
Thompson, Col. Perronet, notices of, 191, 214
Thru Tracts on Spanish and Portuguese Affairs, 190
Tooke, Home, reference to, 54, 194
Townsend, the Rev. Joseph, 212
Trade, how regulated, 107, 195
Trail, James, 96, 132
Traitis de Ligislation, 137
Transplanting laws, 202
Transportation as a punishment, 39
Truth versus *Ashhurst,* 127
Uncertainty in punishments, 145
Universal Grammar, 173
Universal Suffrage, 162, 176
University of Oxford, 13, 174
Usury, defence of, 82
Usury laws, account of the, 80
Utility, the principle of, 20, 29, 30, 31, 36, 141, 212, 216
Vagrants, treatment of, 133
Valuation of pleasure and pain, 213
Venezuela, proposal of Bentham to

visit, 168
Vengeance, avoidance of, in punishment, 140
Vernon, Miss, 45, 117
Voltaire: translation of his *Taureau Blanc,* by Bentham, 34
Voltaire, influence of, on Bentham's style, 35
Voting. See *Suffrage*
Wallas, Graham, *Life of Francis Place* by, cited *passim*
War, Bentham's hatred of, 100
Warwick, Bentham's visit to Castle of, 118
Wedderburn, Alex. (Lord Loughborough, afterwards Earl of Rosslyn), 40, 41, 58-60
Wellington, Duke of, 202, 203
Westminster School, 12, 13
Westminster Elections. *SeeBurdett*
Westminster Review, 191
White, Blanco, 150
Wilberforce, William, 86, 101, 110
Wilkes, John, 17, 18, 23
Wilson, George, 26, 31, 32, 40, 79, 87. 94. 96
Wisdom of our Ancestors, the fallacy as to the, 185
Witnesses, rules as to, 226
Words, coined by Bentham, 27
Workhouses, suggestion as to, 135
Wycombe, Lord, 47, 94, 95, 97
Yewhurst, Bentham's visit to, 18
Young, Arthur, his *Annals of Agriculture,* 135

PLYMOUTH WILLIAM BRENDON AND SON, LIMITED PRINTERS

CPSIA information can be obtained at www.ICGtesting.com
Printed in the USA
BVOW10s1945301214

381363BV00019B/375/P

9 781230 356983